Born in Wiltshire in 1848, Richard Jefferies is now established as a classic writer of the Victorian countryside.
Perhaps only Wordsworth was able to evoke nature in its
many moods and feelings as Jefferies does, but combined
with this lyrical feel for the countryside is an intense interest in the everyday lives of country people, both at
work and at home.

The Toilers of the Field, first published in 1892, brings
together Jefferies' finest work. Whether writing about the
farmer at home, the daily life of a Wiltshire labourer, or of
a typical English homestead, Jefferies creates a unique
historical view of English rural life in the last century and a
delightful picture of the changing rhythms of nature in the
countryside.

The cover shows a detail of 'Wheat' by John Linnell Snr.
Courtesy of Sotheby's Belgravia.

HERITAGE

THE TOILERS OF THE FIELD

Richard Jefferies

Macdonald Futura Publishers

A Futura Book

*First Published in Great Britain
by Longmans, Green, & Co in 1892*

First Futura edition 1981

ISBN 0 7088 2068 9

Photoset by
Rowland Phototypesetting Ltd
Bury St Edmunds Suffolk

Printed and bound in Great Britain by
©ollins, Glasgow

Macdonald Futura Publishers Ltd
Paulton House
8 Shepherdess Walk
London N1 7LW

CONTENTS

Introduction by Victor E. Neuberg

INTRODUCTION

I

Richard Jefferies was born on the 6th November 1848 at Coate Farm near Swindon in Wiltshire. His father, the son of a miller, was a small farmer who could scarcely have anticipated that his farmhouse, which he sold in 1878, would become a museum and a literary shrine* (Open to the public on Wednesday, Saturday and Sunday, 2–5 pm), still less that it would eventually stand, as it does today, on the fringe of a built-up area, only a few yards from a noisy dual carriageway.

When he was four, the boy was sent to stay with an aunt in Sydenham, revisiting Coate for a month's holiday each year. At the age of nine he returned home and went to school in Swindon. In 1944, a contemporary, James Bush, then aged 93, recalled the school that he and Jefferies had attended:

'. . . The schoolmaster's name was Jenkins. To increase his income Mr Jenkins had a private class in which I and Jefferies were pupils. The school was a 2d† fee education—a National School . . . We, as boys of humble

*The building was rescued and restored by Swindon Council in 1926.
†Two old pence—a sum rather less than one new penny.

parentage, looked upon Jefferies as a gentleman's son. He stood aloof from us, never mixing in our games.'*

When he was sixteen, Jefferies and a friend ran away from school and set out for France, intending to walk to Moscow. They changed their plans however, and decided to go to America. Upon reaching Liverpool they realised that they possessed insufficient money and returned home where Jefferies remained for a time until he became a journalist employed by the *North Wiltshire Herald* in 1866. Towards the end of 1867 or early in 1868, he joined the *Wiltshire and Gloucestershire Standard*, and stayed with the paper until 1873.

By this time he had started out as a serious writer and in 1874, his first novel, *The Scarlet Shawl*, was published. It was in this year too that he married Jessie Baden and moved to Swindon. Most of 1875 was spent at Surbiton, and in that year, his second novel, *Restless Human Hearts*, came out. It was followed by a third, *World's End*, in 1877, by which time he was back in Swindon. The three novels were not successful; but with the appearance of *The Gamekeeper at Home*; or, *Sketches of Natural History and Rural Life* in 1878, his reputation as a serious writer about nature was established.

During the nine years of life that remained to him, Jefferies published a stream of books and articles, much of it written while he was in bad health. He became seriously ill in 1881, but his creative energy was undiminished. For the last two years of his life unable to hold a pen, he dictated to his wife who acted as his *amanuensis*. The last

* Quoted in S. J. Looker and C. Porteous, *Richard Jefferies Man of the Fields* 1964 Page 19.

years were passed in Sussex; and his son, Harold, wrote of this period:

> 'My memories at least those intimately connected with my father at Goring, are very sparse, owing to him being mostly confined to his room where my mother took his dictation in longhand. His health at the time did not allow him to take long walks. In fact I do not remember that he ever came down to the solitary beach with me.'*

It was at Goring that he died aged 38, on the 14th August, 1887. His wife, who had nursed him devotedly through a long and trying illness, survived him by nearly forty years and died in 1926.

Omitting the early novels, books on local history, some pamphlets and unpublished MSS, the following is a list of Jefferies most important works:-

The Gamekeeper at Home	1878
Wild Life in a Southern County	1879
The Amateur Poacher	
Green Ferne Farm	
Hodge and His Masters	1880
Round about a Great Estate	
Wood Magic	1881
Bevis	1882
Nature Near London	1883
The Story of My Heart	
Red Deer	1884
The Life of the Fields	
The Dewy Morn	

*Looker and Porteous op. cit. pp. 202–203

II

With Jefferies' life sketched in brief outline, two things remain to be done. It is necessary first to indicate the tradition of rural writing within which he worked and then to see how *THE TOILERS OF THE FIELD* fitted in to it.

The tradition of rural writing in England is a curiously neglected topic. There are, it is true, excellent studies of individual authors (H. Coombes, *Edward Thomas*, 1956 for example): but in general terms the literature of the countryside is not, and indeed never has been, regarded as a discrete field of study. Why should this be so? It is arguable, on the one hand, that the subject is too vaguely defined, and on the other, that it falls too easily between several traditionally accepted areas of academic interest. It is also true that attention tends to be focussed upon major figures like Hardy or Wordsworth. The most cogent reason, however, seems to me to lie within the uneven nature of country writing. The writer may be a novelist, poet, essayist, naturalist, agricultural commentator, folk-lorist, rural sociologist, historian . . . (Jefferies, in fact, was nearly all of these at one time or another.)

There is also the problem of "minor" writers. It has often been difficult to identify them, to get hold of their books outside major libraries, and above all to fit them adequately into a literary or historical discussion. Undoubtedly, many of them have been important in the making of a rural tradition in literature. Thomas Miller, for example, a long forgotten early nineteenth-century author wrote some splendid books about the countryside; and at about the same time, there was William Howitt, whose *The Rural Life of England*, first published in 1838, still awaits rediscovery by the twentieth century. The list could be extended at great length, but what is certain is the existence of a rich and many-sided tradition of English country writing. It stretches—and I am thinking here only of major figures—from Izaak Walton through Gilbert White, Wordsworth, Cobbett, Borrow, Jefferies, Hardy, George Sturt . . . down to Flora Thompson and M. K. Ashby.* Three critics† have recently made forays into the subject and each one, in a rather different way, has provided fresh insights and new ways of looking at the rural tradition.

Running through it, there are two main threads. One very much the rarer, is that of nature mysticism; the other, which is a great deal commoner, though equally hard to do well, is that of observation and comment. Jefferies is unique amongst the country writers, not simply because he was equally at home with both (the same might be said of Wordsworth or Edward Thomas), but because he alone possessed to a remarkable degree the ability to disassociate one from the other. How else could he have written *The Story of My Heart* or *Hodge and His Masters*?

It is this artistic gift plus an extraordinary versatility which makes Jefferies hard to classify as a writer. Clearly

*See Further Reading
†Namely W. J. Keith, Merryn Williams and Raymond Williams. See Further Reading.

Gilbert White excelled him as a naturalist, and Hardy was a greater novelist; but only Wordsworth was able to evoke nature in its many moods and feelings as Jefferies does. At the same time, he wrote about pig-keeping, butter-making, farm machinery, the care of sporting guns, and meat prices. Indeed, he wandered over the Wiltshire Downs with a gun under his arm, not to use it, but to persuade the world in general that he was a practical man whose head was not in the clouds. Jefferies was dazzled by nature, and he fits readily into the broad tradition of countryside writing. At the same time he was, as Raymond Williams has pointed out, 'a major contributor to the social history of rural England.'[*]

His contribution was made mainly in two books, *Hodge and His Masters* (1880) and *The Toilers of the Field* (1892). Both books grew out of Jefferies' journalism. The greater part of *Hodge* was made up a series of articles which he had contributed to the *Wiltshire and Gloucestershire Standard* in the early 1870s. The making of *The Toilers* was rather different: it comprised a number of pieces that had first appeared in *Fraser's Magazine* during 1874 and there were some letters on 'Wiltshire Labourers' which had been written to *The Times* in 1872 during a controversy which centred around Joseph Arch and his attempts to form a labour trades union for agricultural workers. There was also a hitherto unpublished short story and in Part II, five brief, though entirely characteristic essays which appeared in *Longman's Magazine* after Jefferies' death.

Hodge has been reprinted several times. The best edition, I think, was the one revised by Henry Williamson.[†] It

[*] *The Country and the City* (1973) p. 192
[†] Published in 1937

was a confident revision. Williamson, himself a great admirer of Jefferies, wrote in the foreword:

'I believe that if Jefferies had lived beyond his 38 years . . . and been a whole man for the natural span, he would have recast his books as I have done. For always his idea in writing was to recreate what had happened in space and time: to make an elemental picture of the country he knew best—Wiltshire—and to give life to its people.'*

By the time *Hodge* was published, Jefferies was fairly well established as a writer. It would be tempting and not altogether misleading to regard this book as a kind of rural equivalent of Henry Mayhew's massive survey of the London poor (both writers, after all, were journalists, both had enquiring minds, and both were moved by what they saw). Jefferies' work is on a very much smaller scale, and occasionally, as Raymond Williams has said, 'he wrote what his readers wanted to hear'.†

Against this we have to balance the shrewdness of his observations and the deft way in which he moves between the people he writes about and their way of life.

The Toilers of the Field, written after *Hodge*, is a less discursive book and has, for the most part, a sharper focus. The first five pieces, which take up more than half the book, have a unity and a tautness that the earlier book lacks. *The Times* letters, written as an intervention against Arch, possess a directness, a coherence and even a muter note of polemic. Part I of *The Toilers* shows us a Jefferies with a deeper and more controlled perception of the rural

*Op. cit. p. v.
†Op. cit. p. 194

poor and their problems than the author of *Hodge*. It was a
perception almost certainly heightened by the physical
evidence of Swindon's growth and increasing importance
both as a railway junction and as a repair depot. Invasion of
the countryside by the new technology seems to have
added a new dimension to Jefferies' vision. The problems
of rural life were made more difficult.

'Though in the midst of a country teeming with milk, it
is often with the utmost difficulty that she (ie the
labourer's wife) can obtain any for her babe, if nature
shall have rendered her dependent upon an artificial
supply. This has become especially the case of late years,
now that so much milk is sent to London instead of
being retained in the dairy for the manufacture of butter
and cheese . . . No one cares to retail a pennyworth of
milk.'*

Jefferies wrote about country women with no trace of
sentiment. In the letters to *The Times*, flawed as they are,
perhaps, by hostility to the cause Arch was promoting, he
was still able to see both sides of a moral question, and to
write of country women with sympathy.

'As a rule, it may safely be laid down that the agricultural women are moral, far more so than those of the
town. Rough and rude jokes and language are, indeed,
too common; but that is all. No evil comes of it. The
fairs are the chief cause of immorality. Many an honest,
hard-working servant girl owes her ruin to these fatal
mops and fairs, when liquor to which she is unaccustomed overcomes her. Yet it seems cruel to take from

The Toilers of the Field 1901 Edition p. 113

them the one day or two of the year on which they can enjoy themselves fairly in their own fashion.'*

He goes on to advocate friendly societies patronised by the gentry and the clergy as a remedy against immorality. Yet it would be unfair to Jefferies to expect him to see the problems of the poor and their solution through eyes other than those of the farmer. What is surprising is that he transcends this view often. Indeed much of this book invites comparison with Thomas Hardy's study *The Dorsetshire Labourer†*, which probably owed a good deal to Jefferies—of whom we sometimes catch an echo in Hardy's prose:

> 'Drudgery in the slums and alleys of a city, too long pursued, and accompanied as it too often is by indifferent health, may induce a mood of despondency which is well-nigh permanent; but the same degree of drudgery in the fields results at worst in a mood of painless passivity.'‡

The five short pieces which make up Part II of *The Toilers* demonstrate both the quality of his nature writing and also the ways in which the perception of nature both enhanced and extended his awareness of the changing human condition. The sharpness of his eye is beyond doubt. Look, for example, at the opening paragraph of *The Coming of Summer* in this book. Its simplicity is deceptive. Or savour the short essay *Orchis Mascula*, with its undertones of a continuing tradition. This was how Jefferies saw history; he explored the relationship between people and

*Ibid p. 227
†First published in *Longman's Magazine* July 1883 Reprinted in H. Orel, Editor, *Thomas Hardy's Personal Writings*, 1967.
‡Orel op. cit. p. 171.

the countryside. His acute sensitivity to the changing rhythms of human life, the seasons, plants, trees, animals, the shape of the fields, the work of craftsmen, the inner life of men and women, come together to create a unique historical view of the countryside.

The Toilers of the Field has long been out of print, although it had been reprinted five times by 1901. It has been to a considerable extent overshadowed by some of its writer's other works, a few of which are still in print, yet it demonstrates perhaps better than any of his books the intensity and uniqueness of his historical vision.

III
FURTHER READING

Biography
Edward Thomas, *Richard Jefferies* (London 1978). This is a reprint of a standard biography first published in 1909 as *Richard Jefferies: his Life and Work*. It should be read in conjunction with Samuel Looker and Crichton Porteous, *Richard Jefferies Man of the Fields* (London 1964).

Criticism
W. J. Keith, *Richard Jefferies: a Critical Study* (Toronto and London, 1965). A detailed work which contains a near-complete list of secondary sources up to the time of publication.

The same author's *The Rural Tradition* (Hassocks, 1975) sets Jefferies firmly within the context of English country writing.

Also useful are Raymond Williams, *The Country and The City* (London, 1973) and Merryn Williams, *Thomas Hardy and the Rural Tradition* (London, 1972).

Rural Background

The number of titles is enormous. Among them, I have found the following both useful and suggestive. G. E. Mingay, *Rural Life in Victorian England* (London, 1976) is brief, authoritative and contains a substantial bibliography which, curiously enough, does not include *The Toilers of the Field*.

In the 'History Workshop Series', *Village Life and Labour*, Edited by R. Samuel (London, 1975), contains four rigorous, well documented essays on different aspects of rural life.

Amongst older books W. Hasbach, *A History of the English Agricultural Labourer* (London, 1908. Reprinted 1966), is still useful.

E. C. Pulbrook, *English Country Life and Work* (No date. London, *c.*1922. Reprinted 1976) is an unjustly neglected minor classic of the countryside. So too is Richard Heath, *The English Peasant* (London, 1893).

Finally a beautifully written and superbly unsentimental view of rural life. M. K. Ashby in a life of her father, *Joseph Ashby of Tysoe 1859–1919* (Cambridge, 1961. Reprinted London, 1974), has produced a book in which artistry and authenticity combine to produce a memorable study.

Two further books of interest, one just published and one about to be published at the time of writing this Introduction, are:

1 Denys Thompson (Ed), *Change and Tradition in Rural England* (Cambridge University Press, 1980).
2 Gordon F. Mingay (Ed), *The Victorian Countryside* (two volumes, Routledge & Kegan Paul, Summer 1981).

VICTOR E NEUBERG

PART ONE

THE FARMER AT HOME

THE new towns, or suburbs which spring up every year in the neighbourhood of London, are all built upon much the same plan. Whole streets of houses present exact duplicates of each other, even to the number of steps up to the front door and the position of the scraper. In the country, where a new farmhouse is erected about once in twenty years, the styles of architecture are as varied and as irregular as in town they are prim and uniform. The great mass of farmhouses are old, and some are very picturesque. There was a farmhouse I knew which was almost entitled to be taken as the type of an English rural homestead. It was built at a spot where the open wild down suddenly fell away into rich meadow land. Here there was a narrow steep-sided valley, or 'combe'—and at the mouth of this, well sheltered on three sides from the north, the east, and north-eastern winds, stood the homestead. A spring arose some way behind, and close to the house widened into a pool which was still further enlarged by means of a dam, forming a small lake of the clearest water. This lake fed a mill-race lower down. The farmyard and rick-barton were a little way up the narrow valley, on one side of which there was a rookery. The house itself was built in the pure Elizabethan style; with mullioned windows, and innumerable gables roofed with tiles. Nor was it wanting in the traditions of the olden time. This fine old place was the homestead of a large farm comprising some of the best land of the district, both down and meadow. Another farmhouse, still used for that purpose, stands upon the wildest part of the down, and is built of flint and concrete. It was erected nearly three hundred years ago, and is of unusual size. The woodwork is all solid black oak, good enough for an earl's mansion.

These are specimens of the highest class of farmhouse. Immediately beneath them come the houses built in the early part of the present century. They vary in almost every architectural detail, and the materials differ in each county; but the general arrangement is the same. They consist as it were of two distinct houses under one roof. The front is the dwelling-house proper, usually containing a kitchen, sitting-room, and parlour. The back contains the wood-house (coal-house now), the brewhouse— where the beer was brewed, which frequently also had an oven—and, most important of all, the dairy. All this part of the place is paved with stone flags, and the dairy is usually furnished with lattice-work in front of the windows, so that they can be left open to admit the cool air and not thieves. Coolness is the great requisite in a dairy, and some gentlemen who make farming a science go to the length of having a fountain of water constantly playing in it. These houses, however, were built before scientific agriculture was thought of. The wood-house contained the wood used for cooking and domestic purposes; for at that date wood was universally used in the country, and coal rarely seen. The wood was of course grown on the farm, for which purpose those wide double mound hedges, now rapidly disappearing, were made. It was considered a good arrangement to devote half-an-acre in some outlying portion of the farm entirely to wood, not only for the fire, but for poles, to make posts and rails, gates, ladders, &c. The coal could not in those days be conveyed so cheaply as it now is by railways. Such as was used had to be brought by the slow barges on the canals, or else was fetched by the farmers' waggons direct from the pit-mouth. The teams were not unfrequently absent two days and a night on the journey. In the outlying districts this difficulty in obtaining coal practically restricted the available fuel to wood. Now the wood-house is used as much for coal as wood. Of course the great stacks of wood—the piles of faggots and logs—were kept outside, generally in the same enclosure as the ricks, only a sufficient number for immediate use being kept under cover. The brewhouse was an important feature when all farmers brewed their own beer and baked their own bread. At present the great majority purchase their beer from the brewers, although some still brew large quantities for the labourer's drinking in harvest time. At a period when comparatively little ready money passed between employer and employed, and the payment for work was made in kind, beer was a matter which required a great deal of the attention of the farmer, and absorbed no little of his time. At this day it is a disputed matter which is cheapest, to buy or brew beer: at that time there was no question about it. It was indisputably economical to brew. The brewhouse was not necessarily confined to that use; when no brewing was in progress it was often made a kind of second dairy. Over these offices was the cheese-room. This was and still is a long, large, and lofty room in which the cheese after being made is taken to dry and harden. It is furnished with a number of shelves upon which the cheeses are arranged, and as no two can be placed one on the other in the early stage of their maturing, much space is required. It is the duty of the dairymaid and her assistant to turn these cheeses every morning—a work requiring some strength. In this part of the house are the servants' rooms. In front of the dairy and brewhouse is a paved court enclosed with a wall, and in this court it was not uncommon to find a well, or hogtub, for the refuse of the dairy. Sometimes, but not often now, the pig-stye is just outside the wall which surrounds the court. In this court, too, the butter is generally churned, under a 'skilling' which covers half of it. Here also the buckets are washed, and other similar duties performed. The labourers come here to receive their daily allowance of beer.

Most farmhouses in large arable farms were originally built so as to have a small dairy at the back; though there was a time when the arable farmer never thought of keeping a cow, and butter and cheese were unknown, except as luxuries, in his establishment. This was during the continuance of the Corn Laws, when everything was sacrificed to the one great object of growing wheat. It was not impossible in those days to find a whole parish (I know of one myself) in which there was not a single cow. Now the great object is meat, then it was corn. But at the time when most of the farmhouses were erected, the system of agriculture pursued was a judicious mixture of the dairy and the cornfield, so that very few old farmhouses exist which have not some form of dairy attached. In the corn-growing times, most of the verdant meadows now employed to graze cattle, or for producing hay, were ploughed up. This may be seen by the regular furrows, unmistakable evidences of the plough. When corn declined in price through the influx of foreign produce, the land was again laid down in grass, and most of it continues so till this hour. It might be roughly estimated that England now contains a third more meadow land than in the early part of the present century, notwithstanding the attempt to plough up the downs.

We now come to the third class of farmsteads—low thatched buildings, little better than large cottages, and indeed frequently converted into dwellings for labourers. These are generally found on small farms, and in districts where there are a number of small landed proprietors. These freeholders built houses according to their means. In process of time they were bought up by the great landowners, and the farms thrown together, when the houses were used for other purposes. Some may still be found, especially in dairy districts. In these the principal part of the house is usually the dairy, which absorbs at least half of the ground floor, and opens on the kitchen, in which the family sit, and in which their food is often cooked. The eaves of the house are low, and there are scarcely any appliances for comfort. The yeomen who originally lived in these places in all respects resembled the labourers with whom they ate and drank and held the most familiar intercourse. Their labourers even slept in the same bedrooms as the family. But these men, though they mingled so freely with the labourer, were his worst enemy. The little profit they made was entirely accumulated by careful economy. They were avaricious and penurious to the last degree, and grudged every halfpenny to the labouring man. They were, and the remnant of them still are, the determined opponent of all progress. The interior of some of these cottage-farmsteads, which still exist, is almost Dutch-like in simplicity and homeliness. The fireplace is of a vast size, fitted with antique iron dogs for burning wood, and on it swing the irons to

sustain the great pot. On each side, right under the
chimney, are seats, the ingle-nook of olden times. The
chimney itself is very large, being specially built for the
purpose of curing sides of bacon by smoking. The
chimneypiece is ornamented with a few odd figures in
crockery-ware, half-a-dozen old brass candlesticks, and
perhaps a snuff-box or tobacco dish. The floor is composed of stone flags—apt to get slimy and damp when the
weather is about to change—and the wide chinks between
them are filled with hardened dirt. In the centre there is a
piece of carpet on which the table stands, but the rest of the
room is bare of carpeting, except the hearth-rug. The low
window has a seat let into the wall under it. The furniture
of the apartment is utilitarian in the strictest sense. There is
nothing there for ornament or luxury, or even for ease;
only what is absolutely necessary. Generally there is a
dresser, above which, on shelves, the dishes and plates are
arranged. A tall upright eight-day clock, with a brazen
face, and an inscription which tells that it was manu-
factured in a neighbouring village, stands in one corner,
and solemnly ticks in its coffin-like panelled case. On each
side of the fireplace there is an arm-chair, often cushioned
with a fox or badger skin, and a great brazen warming-pan
hangs near the door. There is no ceiling properly so called.
These old houses were always built with a huge beam, and
you can see the boards of the floor above, which are merely
white-washed. A fowling-piece, once a flint-lock, now
converted to the percussion cap system, hangs against the
beam, and sometimes dried herbs may be seen there too.
The use of herbs is, however, going out of date. In the
evening when the great logs of wood smoulder upon the
enormous hearth and cast flickering shadows on the walls,
revealing the cat slumbering in the ingle-nook, and the dog

blinking on the rug—when the farmer slowly smokes his long clay pipe with his jug of ale beside him, such an interior might furnish a good subject for a painter. Let the artist who wishes to secure such a scene from oblivion set to work speedily, for these things are fast fading away.

All these three classes of farmhouse are usually well supplied with vegetables from the garden attached. The garden in fact was, and still is, an object of considerable importance to the farmer, quite as much as the allotment to the labourer. He reckons to receive from it his whole supply of potatoes, cabbages, beans, peas, and other varieties of table vegetables, and salads. These constitute an important item when there is a large family. I do not speak now of the great farmers, although even these set some store by such produce, but the middle class. It is usual in these gardens to grow immense quantities of cabbage of a coarse kind, and also of lettuce, onions, and radishes, all of which are freely given to the men and women working on the place during the harvest. They are, in fact, grown especially for them. At the dinner-hour one or more men of the number, deputed by the rest, come up to the house. One carries the wooden bottles, or small barrels of ale, which are handed out from the dairy. The other repairs to the garden, and pulls up a reasonable quantity of lettuce, onions, or radishes, as the case may be, from the patches indicated to him by the employer. These are then washed in the court by the dairy, where there is almost always a pump, and are then taken out to the men and shared amongst them. These salads make an agreeable addition to the dry bread and cheese, or bacon. The custom is an old one, and much to be commended. It costs the employer next to nothing, and is an element in that goodwill which should exist between him and the labourer.

On some farms large quantities of fruit are grown—such as gooseberries, currants, plums, and damsons. Most have enough for their own use; some sell a considerable amount. Outside the garden is the orchard. Some of these orchards are very extensive, even in districts where cider is not the ordinary beverage, and in a good apple year the sale of the apples forms an important item in the peculiar emoluments of the farmer's wife. There are, of course, many districts in which the soil is not adapted to the apple, but as a rule the orchard is an adjunct of the garden. Some of the real old English farmsteads possess the crowning delight of a filbert walk, but these are rare now. In fact the introduction of machinery and steam, and the general revolution which has been going on in agriculture, has gone far to sweep away these more pleasant and home-like features of the farm. It becomes daily more and more like a mere official residence, so to speak. The peculiar home-like aspect of a farmhouse is gradually disappearing.

The daily life of the middle-class dairy farmer begins at five in the morning. Rising about that hour, his first duty is to see that the men have all appeared, and that they are engaged in milking the cows. He breakfasts at six, or half-past, and the whole family have finished breakfast before seven. By this time the day-labourers have come (the milkers are usually hired by the year), and the master has to go out and put them on to their jobs. Meantime the dairy is a scene of work and bustle; cheesemaking being in full swing. This is at least superintended, if not partly performed, by the mistress of the house. At larger farms it is the bailiff who rises early and sees that the labourers are properly employed; and the cheesemaking is entrusted to a dairymaid hired at high wages, who often combines with that duty the office of general housekeeper. It was once the practice to rise even earlier than five, but there are not many farmers who do so now. On the arable farm, which is generally much larger, the master has almost always got a bailiff, or head-carter, whom he can trust to see the men set to work. The master is therefore not obliged to come down so soon, except at important seasons. But the ordinary dairy-farm is not large enough to support a bailiff, and the master has to rise himself. The fresh morning air and the exercise give the farmer a tremendous appetite for breakfast. The usual staple food consists of thick rashers of bacon only just 'done', so as to retain most of the fat, the surplus of which is carefully caught on slices of bread. The town rasher is crisp, curled, and brown, without a symptom of fat or grease. The farmer's early rasher is to a town eye but half-done, bubbling with grease, and laid on thick slices of bread, also saturated with the gravy. Sometimes cold bacon is preferred, but it is almost always very fat. With this he drinks a pint or so of fairly strong beer, and afterwards has a hunch of bread and butter and a cup or two of tea. He is then well fortified for the labour of the morning. This is the common breakfast of the working-farmer, who is as much a labouring man as any cottager on his farm, and requires a quantity of solid food. Some, however, who are pretty well off, and have a better idea of the luxuries of the table, regale themselves on collared head, or rolled beef, or ham at breakfast. These hams are usually preserved after a family receipt, and some of them are exquisite. After breakfast the farmer walks round the place, watches the men at work for a few minutes, and gives them instructions, and then settles himself down to some job that requires his immediate superintendence. If it is hay-time he takes a rake and works about the field, knowing full well all the difference that his presence makes.

The agricultural labourers, both men and women, are a slow set, never in a hurry; there is none of that bustle characteristic of the town people, even of the lowest class. They take every opportunity of leaning upon the prong-handle, or standing in the shade—they seem to have no idea of time. Women are a sore trial to the patience of the agriculturist in a busy time. If you want to understand why, go and ensconce yourself behind a hedge, out of sight but in view of a field in which ten or twelve women are hoeing. By and by a pedlar or a van comes slowly along the turnpike road which runs past the field. At the first sound of footsteps or wheels all the bent backs are straight in an instant, and all the work is at a standstill. They stand staring at the van or tramp for five or six minutes, till the object of attention has passed out of sight. Then there is a little hoeing for three or four consecutive minutes. By that time one of them has remembered some little bit of gossip, and stops to tell her nearest fellow-workwoman, and the rest at once pause to listen. After a while they go on again. Now another vehicle passes along the road, and the same process of staring has to be gone through once more. If a lady or gentleman pass, the staring is something terrific, and it takes quite ten minutes to discuss all the probabilities as to who they were, and where they were going. This sort of thing goes on all day, so that, in point of fact, they only do half a day's work. The men are not so bad as this; but they never let slip an opportunity for pausing in their work, and even when at work they do it in a slow, dawdling, lack-energy way that is positively irritating to watch. The agriculturist has in consequence plenty to do to keep his eye on them, and in the course of the day he walks over his farm half-a-dozen times at least. Very few ordinary

working farmers walk much less than ten miles a day on
the average, backwards and forwards over the fields.

Half-past eleven used to be luncheon time, but now it is
about twelve, except in harvest, when, as work begins
earlier, it is at eleven. This luncheon hour is another source
of constant irritation to the agriculturist. He does not wish
to bind his men down to an exact minute, and if a man has
some distance to walk to his cottage, will readily make all
allowance. He does not stint the beer carried out either
then or in the field. But do what he likes, be as considerate
as he will, and let the season be never so pressing, it is
impossible to get the labourers out to their work when the
hour is up. Most of them go to sleep, and have to be waked
up, after which they are as stupid as owls for a quarter of an
hour. One or two, it will be found, have strolled down to
the adjacent ale-house, and are missing. These will come
on the field about an hour later. Then one man has a rake
too heavy for him, and another a prong too light. There is
always some difficulty in starting to work; the agriculturist must therefore be himself present if he wishes to
get the labourers out to the field in anything like a moderate time.

The nuisance of mowers must be gone through to be
appreciated. They come and work very well for the first
week. They slash down acre after acre, and stick to it
almost day and night. In consequence the farmer puts on
every man who applies for work, everything goes on
first-rate, and there is a prospect of getting the crop in
speedily. At the end of the week the mowers draw their
money, quite a lump for them, and away they go to the
ale-house. Saturday night sees them as drunk as men can
be. They lie about the fields under the hedges all day
Sunday, drinking when the public-house is open. Monday

morning they go on to work for half-an-hour, but the fever engendered by so much liquor, and the disordered state of the stomach, cause a burning thirst. They fling the scythes down, and go off to the barrel. During all this week perhaps between them they manage to cut half an acre. What is the result? The haymakers have made all the grass that was cut the first week into hay, and are standing about idle, unable to proceed, but still drawing their wages from the unfortunate agriculturist. The hot sun is burning on—better weather for haymaking could not be—but there is not a rood of grass cut for them to work on. After a while the mowers come back, thoroughly tired and exhausted with their debauch, and go on feebly to work. There is hope again. But our climate is notoriously changeable. A fortnight of warm, close heat is pretty sure to breed a thunderstorm. Accordingly, just as the scythes begin to lay the tall grass prostrate again, there is a growl in the sky, and down comes the rain. A thunderstorm unsettles the weather, and here is perhaps another week lost. The farmer dares not discharge his haymakers, because he does not know but that he may require them any day. They are put to turn dungheaps, clean out the yards, pick up the weeds in the garden, and such like little jobs, over which they can dawdle as much as they like. All the while they are on full pay. Now, what manufacturer could endure such conduct as this? Is it not enough to drive a saint out of his patience? Of course the larger farmers who can afford it have the resource of the mowing-machine, but there are hundreds and thousands of farms upon which its sharp rattle has not yet been heard. There is still a great divergence of opinion as to its merits, many maintaining that it does not cut so close to the ground, and therefore wastes a large percentage of the crop, and others that the action of the scissor-like knives bruises the grass, and prevents it growing up into a good after-math. Therefore many farmers who could afford it will not admit the mowing-machine into their fields, and the mowers may still be seen at work over miles and miles of meadow, and are still the plague of the agriculturist. The arable farmer has just the same difficulty to keep his labourers at their work, and unless he is constantly on the watch valuable time is lost daily. In the harvest, however, he has an advantage. The corn is reaped by piece-work, and the labourers therefore strain every nerve to do as much as they can. But then he must be on the lookout to see that they do not 'scamp' it.

The traditional bacon and greens dinner is passing away, though still the usual fare in the small farmhouses. Most of the fairly well-to-do farmers have a joint twice or three times a week, well supported with every kind of vegetable. There is no attempt at refinement in cooking, but there is plenty of good substantial food.

The hill farmer, whose staple is sheep and wool, has generally a great deal of walking or riding to get over in the day. The down farms are sometimes very large, running perhaps in long narrow strips of land for two or three miles. Although he employs a head-shepherd, and even a bailiff, he finds it necessary, if he would succeed in making a profit, to be pretty well ubiquitous. They all want looking after sharply. Not that there is much actual dishonesty; but would any manufacturer endure to have his men sitting doing nothing on their benches for fifteen minutes out of every hour of the working day, just because his back was turned? The hill farmer has, perhaps, a preferable life in some respects to the agriculturist in the vale. He has not so much actual manual labour to get through. On the other hand, he is at a great distance from any town, or even large village; he sees no one during the day, and he has to run great risks. Wool may fall, so may the price of mutton, either of which would derange his calculations; or the fly may destroy his turnips, or the season may be exceptionally dry and unfavourable. His house is lonely, perched on the side of a hill, and exposed to the bitter blasts of winter which sweep over the downs with resistless fury, and which no doors nor windows can exclude. If there should be snow, it is sure to fall in greater quantities on the hills, and, driving before the wind, fills up the hollows, till the roads are impassable for weeks.

Taking all the year round, the work of the agriculturist begins and ends with the rising and setting of the sun. There is an exception, because the cows must be milked and foddered nearly as early in the winter, when the sun rises very late, as at other seasons; but then, to make up for that, work ends earlier in the afternoon. In the spring, as the evenings draw out, there is almost always something to be done even after the labourers have left. In harvest time, the superintendence of work continues till late, and in the autumn labour is not unfrequently prolonged into the moonlight. In order to carry the corn. It is a life, on the whole, of hard work.

In all this I speak of the ordinary middle-class farmer. The life of the higher class of agriculturists, who possess large capital, and employ bailiffs and all kinds of machinery, is of course not by any means so onerous. It is in general character pretty much that of an independent gentleman, with the addition of the sporting element, and a certain freedom from drawing-room trammels.

To get at the physique of the agriculturists, the best plan is to pay a visit to the market-town. Here almost every farmer in the neighbourhood, no matter of what class—highest, middle, or lowest—is nearly sure to be seen on market-days. The upper class come in in their smart waggonettes, or dog-carts, drawn by thoroughly good and stylish horses, which are little, if at all, inferior to those of the gentry. Some of these keep their groom and coachman, who dress in livery of a quiet and subdued kind, but still unmistakably a livery. The middle-class come in in traps, or old-fashioned four-wheelers, generally bringing their wives and daughters, to do the shopping of the week. The market-day is, in fact, the event of the week, and the streets of the market-town are the Rotten Row of the neighbourhood. The wives and daughters come in their best dresses, and promenade up and down, and many a flirtation goes on with the young bucks of the district. The lower class of farmers jog in on their mares, rough as cart-horses, and the rider generally so manages to seat himself as to show three or four inches of stocking between his trousers and boots. After the market is over, and the dealing done, the farmers resort to the various inns, and dine at the market ordinary. A very good dinner is usually provided at a low charge on these days. Soup is not usual, the dinner generally beginning with fish, followed by joints, and fowl of various kinds. Wine 'whips' are formed, and the sherry circulates freely. There is a regular chairman, always a man of property and influence, and an old frequenter of the place. After dinner they sit an hour or two discussing, not only the price of sheep and wool or mutton, but the political and other events of the day. The Chambers of Agriculture are generally so arranged as to meet on market-days, about an hour after the ordinary finishes, and not unfrequently in the same room. The market-towns derive great benefit from this habit of congregating on the market–day. It is the day, too, for paying visits by the ladies. Gay costumes pass through the streets, and bright eyes look out of the windows of the hotels upon the crowd of farmers. The yards of the various hostelries are made almost impassable by the innumerable variety of vehicles. The young farmers take the opportunity of playing a game at billiards, which they rarely do on other days. The news of the whole countryside is exchanged, and spreads from mouth to mouth, and is carried home and sent farther on its way. One great characteristic is the general good-humour that prevails. The laugh and the joke are frequently heard—it is a kind of moderate gala-day. The fishmonger's shop is emptied, and the contents carried home, this being the only day in the week when fish is bought by the majority of agriculturists. Some towns have only what is called a 'gin-and-water' market: that is, the 'deal' is begun and concluded from small samples carried in the pocket and examined at an inn over a glass of spirits and water. But in the great market-towns there is now almost always a large room, or hall, set aside for this special purpose. The market begins and concludes at a fixed time, indicated by the ringing of a bell. In this hall the dealers have stands, furnished with desks, at which they may always be found, and here sacks of samples are pitched. There is a clerk of the market, and the current prices are posted up, and afterwards sent to all the local newspapers. The cattle-market used to be carried on entirely in the streets, each farmer selling his own beasts or sheep by private treaty with the dealers. The streets were then often filled with cattle from one end to the other, and were almost impassable for vehicles, and at times not a little dangerous for foot-passengers. Now the practice of selling by auction has become very general, and the cattle are either put into the auctioneer's private yard, or in an enclosure provided by the town authorities. The corn-dealers are a most energetic class of men, well educated, and often employing large capital in their business. They are perpetually travelling, and often attend two markets a day. Having struck a bargain, the farmer and the purchaser adjourn to the hotel, and have a glass of spirits, without which no transaction seems complete. The use of beer has very much declined among the fairly well-to-do agriculturists. They drink it at dinner and lunch, but whenever a glass is taken with a friend, or in calling at an inn, it is almost invariably spirits. Whisky has been most extensively drunk of late years.

No other class of men employing so much capital and so many labourers are so simple in their habits as the agriculturists. In dress they adhere to the plainest colours and shapes; there is no attempt to keep pace with the fashion. The materials of the coat and vest are good, and even expensive, but the cut is old and out of date, and the whole effect quite plain. There is no shirt front, no studs, no rings, no kid gloves. The boots are strong and thick, substantial, but not ornamental. A man with his ten or fifteen thousand perhaps will walk down the street buttoned up in an ungainly greatcoat and an old hat, not half so smartly dressed as a well-paid mechanic, and far behind the drapers' assistants in style. There is a species of contempt among them for the meretricious and showy; they believe in the solid. This very fact makes them good friends to shopkeepers, who have no better customers. They carry this leading idea too far, for they admire an article in precisely a corresponding ratio to the money it costs, totally oblivious of all considerations of art or ornament. The first question invariably is, if they are asked to

admire anything, 'What did it cost?' This results in a heavy
and cumbrous style of furniture even in the best farmsteads.
Everything must be massive, costly, and strong. Artistic
tendencies they have none. They want something durable,
and they get it. But on the whole they make marvellously
little show for their money. Hundreds of the most substantial agriculturists, whose cheques would be honoured
for thousands of pounds, seem absolutely to make no
show at all. At the same time it is quite true that some of
the rising generation, who have very little to do it on,
make a great display with hunters and plated harness, and
so forth. But they are not the rule. The generality go just
the other way, and live below their income, and take a
lower station in society than they might reasonably claim.

Farmers are decidedly a marrying class of men. The
farm is a business in which a wife is of material service, and
can really be a helpmate. The lower class of farmers usually marry quite as much or more for that reason than any
others. The higher classes of agriculturists feel that they
have a right to marry because they too can show a home in
which to keep a wife. Though they may not have any large
amount of capital, still they possess a good house and
sufficient provision. They are, therefore a marrying class
of men, but do not commonly contract matrimonial al-
liances very early in life. The great object of an agriculturist who has sons is to get them settled in farms, and it
is astonishing to what an extent this is carried by men who
do not seem to have much capital to start their children
with. Instances are common in which a man has three or
four sons all in farms, and doing fairly well. One of the
greatest difficulties he has to contend against is the necessity of providing education. Where is a farmer, living
perhaps two or three miles, often enough four and six

miles, from a town, to send his boys to school? The upper class of agriculturists can, of course, afford to have a proper governess at home till they are old enough, and then send them to one of the so-called middle-class schools. The lower class, on the other hand, who do not aspire very high, and whose ideas are little more ambitious than those of their labourers, are contented with the school in the neighbouring village. Till recently these village schools were very poor affairs, something a little better than the old dame school, but not much. But since the new Education Act the lower class of farmers are in a better position with respect to education than those who possess much higher claims to social distinction. Where there is not a school board, the clergyman and the landowners have combined, and built first-rate schools, up to all the requirements of the Act, and attended by properly certified teachers. The lower class farmer, who is troubled with no scruples about the association of his boys with the labourers' children, can send them to this school at a very low charge indeed, and they will there receive a good foundation. But the middle-class farmer—the man who is neither an independent gentleman, nor obliged to live on bacon and greens—is unprovided for, and yet this class is the most numerous. They have better views for their sons than to confine those early impressions upon which so much depends to the narrow and rude, if not coarse manners of the labourers' children. They look higher than that, and they are fully justified in doing so. They do not, therefore, at all relish the idea of sending their boys to the national school of the parish, let it be never so well supplied with teachers. There is another objection to it. It has a faint suspicion of the pauper. Now if there is anything a downright English yeoman abominates more than all the rest it is any approach to the 'parish'. This is a 'parish' school. It is not a paupers' school—that is admitted—but it' is a 'parish' school, to which the children of men who have often received relief are sent. The yeoman's instinct revolts at it. Attempts have been made to get over this niceness of feeling by erecting a special class-room for farmers' sons, and patriotic baronets have even gone so far as to send their own boys so as to set the example. But it is in vain. The middle-class farmer is above all men exclusive in his ideas. He detests the slightest flavour of communism. He likes to be completely and fully independent. He will not patronise the 'parish' school. What then is he to do? At this present moment most farmers' sons are sent into the neighbouring towns to the middle-class schools which are to be found there. If the farmer is within two or three miles the boys walk or ride on ponies every morning. If it is farther than that they go as weekly boarders, and return home every Saturday. The fault in this system is simply and solely in the character of the school. Too often it is a school in name only, where the boys learn next to nothing at all, except mischief. Very few schools exist in these small country towns which afford a good education at a moderate price. It is almost impossible that they should exist without an endowment, as the scholars can never be numerous enough to make the profits exceed the expenditure. The result is that the middle-class farmer cannot give his boys a good education unless he sends them to what is called a middle-class school in some town at a great distance, and this he cannot afford. The sum demanded by these so-called middle-class schools is beyond his reach. He may, perhaps, if he has only one son, indulge in the expensive luxury of a sound and thorough education for him. But if there are several the thing is out of the question. With the girls it is even worse—where can he send them? They cannot very well walk or ride to and fro like the boys to the school in the nearest town, and if they are boarded at such schools, the education given is paltry and meagre in the extreme. A good girls' school is one of the rarest things in the country. The result is that a governess is kept while the girls are young. This governess is under-paid, and has consequently herself been only partially educated. Then as the girls grow older they are sent for a year or two, to 'finish' them, to some young ladies' academy, and the ultimate product is a smattering of French and music, and crude ideas of fashion and refine-ment, which make them dissatisfied with their home and unfit for an agricultural life as the wife of a farmer.

The nonsense talked and published of farmers having pianos, and their daughters strumming all day long instead of attending to the dairy, is perfectly absurd. It is quite true that in hundreds of farmhouses, just at the time when the dairy is in full work in the morning, a piano may be heard going. This is the governess instructing the girls when the farmer is not sufficiently rich to send them to a school. But when once these girls are grown up, and have finished their education, poor as it is, and return home to take a part in the household duties, then the piano is never heard in the morning when work is about. The farmer's wife sees to that sharp enough. In the evening it may be heard—and why not? If the agricultural labourer is to be polished up and refined, why on earth should not his employer take a step in advance? It must be remembered that there is very little society in the country; scarcely any one even passing along the road. There are none of those cheap sights and amusements so readily accessible to the poorest in a great city. The wives and daughters of the mechanics and work-

men in London can once a week at least afford to enjoy
themselves at some theatre or place of amusement. They
are far better off in this respect than the daughters of
agriculturists who may be worth thousands. These have
nothing whatever to amuse themselves with during the
long evenings; they cannot even take a stroll out and look
at the shop windows. They are surely entitled to the
simple and inexpensive amusement of a piano. It is in fact
their only resource. There was a statement in the newspapers of farmers taking their daughters to Paris. It is
possible that some of the upper class of farmers, who are in
fact independent gentlemen, may have done so; but as for
the ordinary middle-class farmers, such a thing is utterly
unheard of. It is very few of them who even take their
wives to London or the seaside for a week. But even if they
did, it is nothing more than they are entitled to do. Half the
tradesmen who do such things do not possess anything
like the income of the farmers. The fact is, that the agriculturists are a singularly stay-at-home race of men. The
great majority never leave their farms to go farther than
the market-town from one year's end to the other. Above
all classes they are attached to their homes, and slow to go
away even temporarily. To such a length is this feeling
carried that men have been known to go partially insane
for a while at the prospect of having to quit a farm through
a landlord's decease, even though no appreciable pecuniary loss was involved.

The agriculturists are a remarkably observant race, and
as a rule peculiarly well-informed. This is contrary to the
popular belief, which represents the farmer as rude and
ignorant, a pot-bellied beer-drinker, and nothing more.
But the popular belief is a delusion. I do not say that they
are literary or scientific in their tastes and private pur-

suits. There are no great names among them in geology, or astonomy, or anthropology, or any other science. They are not artists in any sense. But they are singularly well-informed. They possess more general knowledge than any other class, and can converse on subjects with which townsmen seem unacquainted. Many of them have very fair libraries, not extensive, but containing books of sterling excellence. Farming is necessarily an isolated business—there is little society. Except on market-days, there is scarcely any interchange of conversation. There is, too, at certain seasons of the year a good deal of leisure. What books they own, therefore, are well read, and the contents reflected upon. It is that habit of thinking over what is read that makes all the difference. It is impossible to avoid being struck with the immense amount of general information possessed by some agriculturists, and the wide field over which their knowledge ranges. Yet with all this knowledge and power of reflection they still remain attached to the old-world system of politics, religion, and social relations.

The habits of intemperance which were at one time a just and standing reproach against the agriculturist have almost entirely disappeared. A drunken farmer is now unknown. They are as fond as ever of offering hospitality to a friend, and as ready to take a social glass—no total abstainers amongst them; but the steady hard-drinking sot has passed away. The old dodge of filling the bottle with gin instead of water, and so pouring out pure spirit, instead of spirit and water, when the guests were partially intoxicated, in order to complete the process, is no more known. They do not drink more than the inhabitants of towns.

It is a singular fact that with so many streams and ponds

scattered about the country within easy reach, the farmers do not care for fishing. A farmer engaged in fishing is a rarity indeed. They are eagerly fond of fox-hunting, coursing, and shooting, but fishing is a dead letter. A party will sometimes go out and net a pond, but as for fishing proper, with rod and line, it is almost unknown. Every chance of shooting is eagerly snatched at. In May the young rooks are shot, after which the gun is put aside for a while. At the end of July some of the young rabbits are ready, and are occasionally knocked over. Very few tenant farmers shoot game even when they could do so, leaving that for some neighbouring gentleman with whom they are friendly, and this too without any remuneration, the fact being that winged game does little damage. But they wage unceasing war on the rabbits, with dog and gun and ferret. All the winter long they are hunted in every possible way. This is, of course, on farms where the tenant has permission to kill the rabbits. Whist and post and pair are the staple indoor amusements.

Of all businesses that of agriculture is peculiarly adapted to descend from father to son. In point of fact, farms so frequently pass from the father to the son as to be looked upon almost as a certain inheritance. In agriculture, then, it must be expected that the effects of inherited instincts and ideas should be very plainly shown. From this cause arises the persistent and unreasoning Conservatism of the mass of agriculturists. Out of a list of one hundred farmers, I find that one resides upon a farm which has been in the occupation of members of the same family for three hundred years. He possessed a series of documents, receipts, special agreements, and so on, proving that descent beyond all cavil; but with the usual want of proper appreciation for antiquities, most of these papers have been committed to the flames; still there is no question of the fact, which can still be shown from the landlord's family archives. Nominally that farm has been in the occupation of one family for ten generations, reckoning by the ordinary calculation of thirty years to each. But this average is not fairly applicable to the agricultural life, which is generally long, and occasionally extends into extreme old age. There were probably about eight successors if the line was unbroken; if not, there may of course have been treble that number. A man may be excused some amount of pride when he thinks of such a continuance as this in one spot, for it means not only an exceptional vitality of race, but an exceptional perseverance in the paths of honesty and straightforwardness. But with this pride it also engenders a stubborn unchangeableness, a dislike and hatred of all things new and unfamiliar, a nervous dread of reform. Faithful to the logic of their class, such men as these may in resisting innovations go to lengths which may appear foolish and wrong to others who live in a widely different social atmosphere. To some extent the bitter opposition to change in the position of the labourer, which is thrown in the teeth of the tenant farmer, is the outcome of these very centuries of steady adherence to all that they believed upright and manly.

Another name on my list has been known at one spot for fully two hundred years. These men attained a position beyond that of yeoman, but they never sank beneath it. The rise of many of the great county families really dates from the success of some ancestor, or the collective success of a series of ancestors, in agriculture. They perhaps claim some knight or nobleman as the founder of the race, although he may have really done nothing for the practical advantage of the family; the true founders being merely proprietors of land, dignified as J.P.'s and sometimes sheriffs, throwing off branches into the clerical and legal professions. The real ancestor was the sturdy yeoman who accumulated the money to purchase the farm he tilled, and whose successors had the good sense to go on adding acre to acre till they finally expanded into the wide domains of the modern squire. Not the knight whose effigy in brass paves the aisle of the parish church laid the corner-stone of the wealth and power of to-day, but the shrewd and close-fisted producer and dealer in wool and corn. Their true claim to aristocratic privileges and importance is the sense of centuries of independence. These others of whom we have spoken, the yeoman who never aspired beyond the yeoman's position, are as ancient and as 'worshipful'— to use an old and disused term—as they. I do not instance these descents of three and two hundred years as extraordinary, because I believe that they could be paralleled and even extended by inquiry, but because they came under my own observation. There are others on the list ranging from one hundred and sixty down to sixty and eighty years of continued occupation. But not to go into details, I reckon on an average that thirty names out of a hundred have been the occupiers for three generations; forty for two generations; twenty for one hundred and fifty years; and ten are new comers. But a still more curious and instructive fact is the permanence of certain names over a wide section of country; so much so that in places it is a common saying that one has only to be an A, or a B, or a T, to be certain of getting a farm. Whole parishes seem related, and not very distantly related either; and yet there is not the remotest class-feeling or *esprit de corps*. The isolation and independence of a farm life are powerful agents in preventing anything like cohesion. Any one who will take the trouble to look down the parish register in a strictly agricultural district will be forcibly struck with the permanence of certain names. Page after page contains nothing but records of the marriages, intermarriages, burials, baptisms, and so on of two or three generic names. The population appears to have been stationary for scores upon scores of years. Say what you will, ridicule it as you like, there is a charm clinging round that which time has hallowed; and even the man of the hour, the successful speculator, yields to this. It is his most eager desire to become a landed proprietor, and if possible he buys a place where he can exercise manorial rights.

Taking these things into consideration, it is only reasonable to admit that agriculture is a profession in which a man may, above all others, be excused if he manifests a certain amount of irritability at the prospect of change. The slow round of uneventful years, the long continuance of manual labour, the perpetual iteration of a few ideas, in time produce in the mind of the most powerfully intellectual men a species of unconscious creed; and this creed is religiously handed down from generation to generation. Setting aside those who have gone into agriculture as a science, and adapt everything to commercial principles—and they are as yet not very numerous—the great mass of farmers believe nearly the same now as they did two centuries ago. Looking through a farmer's calendar published in the first few years of this century, and containing a complete *résumé* of the system of agriculture practised then, I was struck by the remarkable fact that in all main features it was the same as that in use now. We have heard so much of the rapid progress of agriculture, of the important changes introduced, and of the complete revolution which has taken place, that this statement may

appear incredible. It is nevertheless the fact that the book
might be put with advantage into the hands of any young
man about to enter upon a farm. With the exception of
those operations which are now performed by steam, and
making an allowance to the altered conditions introduced by the abolition of the Corn Laws, the instructions
given there are useful down to this very day. Here
is the knowledge of the peculiarities and requirements of
stock slowly accumulated during ages of agriculture, and at last written down and printed for easy
reference. However much the aspect of politics may
change, or however much the means of locomotion and
communication may be facilitated by the introduction of
steam, Nature still remains unaltered. The cows and sheep
retain their instincts and their internal economy; their
modes of feeding, times of rest, and seasons of increase,
never vary. The earth too has not changed. The corn is
sown at the same time; Nature goes on her way as before,
heedless of the railway rattle. So it is that the details of
management in this book are as useful now as then, more
than two generations since. It is the same with the unwritten faith of the men who labour and live among these
things. Go out among them, and collect from the majority
their views and sentiments, and in this age of progress they
will be found to correspond almost exactly with those of
their forefathers, as recorded by history. They know that
such is the fact themselves; they know too that it would
subject them to sharp criticism and reproof if they published their real opinions. Therefore they remain
silent, and it is only among themselves that these ideas are
earnestly insisted on.

In the earliest days of agriculture, when Abraham drove
his flocks and herds to and fro under the Syrian sun, the

father of the family was at once the procreator, the law-giver, the judge, the leader in battle, the priest, and the king. He was absolute master under Heaven of all things visible around him. The Pope claims to be infallible now, and to be the vicegerent of Heaven, but the patriarch of old actually possessed those powers upon his own domain. His sons were under his complete control—he could sacrifice them alive to his God if he chose, or banish them from their native land. His daughters were still more completely in his hand, to be done with as he thought fit. His servants, his slaves, were as much his as the wooden pole of his tent, or the very sandals he walked in. They were as dust before him. There was no coming of age in those days; no escape after the twenty-first year. The tie lasted till his death. At forty his sons and daughters were as much his own as they were at ten years old. They tell us that this system, to some extent, still survives in China. In all fundamental points such is the creed of the agricultural race of our own day. Circumstances have, no doubt, had something to do with the production and elaboration of such a faith. In no other profession do the sons and the daughters remain so long, and so naturally, under the parental roof. The growth of half-a-dozen strong sons was a matter of self-congratulation, for each as he came to man's estate took the place of a labourer, and so reduced the money-expenditure. The daughters worked in the dairy, and did not hesitate to milk occasionally, or, at least, to labour in the hayfield. They spun, too, the home-made stuffs in which all the family were clothed. A man's children were his servants. They could not stir a step without his permission. Obedience and reverence to the parent was the first and greatest of all virtues. Its influence was to extend through life, and through the whole social system. They were to choose the wife or the husband approved of at home. At thirty, perhaps, the more fortunate of the sons were placed on farms of their own nominally, but still really under the father's control. They dared not plough or sow except in the way that he approved. Their expenditure was strictly regulated by his orders. This lasted till his death, which might not take place for another twenty years. At the present moment I could point out ten or twelve such cases, where men of thirty or forty are in farms, and to all appearances perfectly free and independent, and yet as completely under the parental thumb as they were at ten years old. Why do they not throw off the burden? Because they have imbibed the same creed, and intend to carry it out in their own persons. These men, if they think thus of their own offspring, cannot be expected to be more tender towards the lower class around them. They did at one time, and some still wish to, extend the same system to the labouring population. As there was in those days little or no work for a man but upon a farm, and as the cottages were chiefly in the hands of the farmers, there was plenty of opportunity for carrying out these ideas. The old method of poor relief gave another handle. They did not want only to indulge in tyranny; what they did was to rule the labouring poor in the same way as they did their own children—nothing more nor less. These labouring men, like his own children, must do as the farmer thought best. They must live here or there, marry so and so, or forfeit favour—in short, obey the parental head. Each farmer was king in his own domain; the united farmers of a parish were kings of the whole place. They did not use the power circumstances gave them harshly; but they paid very little regard to the liberty of the subject. To this very day something of the same sort goes on. It is wonderful with what eager zeal many of the old-style farmers enter into the details of a labourer's life, and carefully ascertain his birth, his parentage, his marriage, his wife's parentage, and the very minutest matters. These facts thus accumulated are talked over in the boardroom when an applicant comes to the union for relief. Very often such special knowledge possessed by a guardian of the antecedents of the applicant is more useful and beneficial in enabling the Board to extend assistance to a deserving man. What I wish to show is the all-permeating influence of the parental system in the mind of the typical agriculturist.

In religion it is, or lately was, the same. It was not a matter with the farmer of the Athanasian creed, or the doctrine of salvation by faith, or any other theological dogma. To him the parish church was the centre of the social system of the parish. It was the keystone of that parental plan of government that he believed in. The very first doctrine preached from the pulpit was that of obedience. 'Honour thy father and thy mother' was inculcated there every seventh day. His father went to church, he went to church himself, and everybody else ought to go. It was as much a social gathering as the dinner at the market ordinary, or the annual audit dinner of their common landlord. The dissenter, who declined to pay church-rates, was an unsocial person. He had left the circle. It was not the theology that they cared about, it was the social nonconformity. In a spiritual sense, too, the clergyman was the father of the parish, the shepherd of the flock—it was a part of the great system. To go a step farther, in political affairs the one leading idea still threaded itself through all. The proper parliamentary representative—the natural lawgiver—was the landlord of the district. He was born amongst them, walked about amongst them, had been in their houses many a time. He knew their wants, their ideas, their views. His own interest was identical with theirs. Therefore he was the man. The logic is indisputable. What is more, they acted up to it. In agricultural districts it is not uncommon even now to find men of diametrically opposite political views to the candidate at an election voting for and supporting him, simply and solely because he is the local man. It is natural and right that he should represent them. That one word 'right' is the key to the whole ethical system of the agriculturists. They cherish and maintain their belief in right, and in their 'rights'—by which they understand much the same thing—even when unaccompanied by any gain or advantage. In brief outline, such is the creed of the agriculturists as a body. It is neither written nor spoken, but it is a living faith which influences every hour of their lives.

This faith must ever be borne in mind by those who wish to understand the movements of the agricultural world. Without making a proper allowance for it, the farmers will be easily misjudged.

The labouring class are imbued to a great extent with the very same ideas. They stick to their rights. They will not give up an old pathway that their fathers used, not if one twice as convenient be offered in lieu of it. They have a right to go that way, and go that way they will. They are brutally tyrannical over their children. I use those words deliberately. He who spares the rod spoils the child, is the practical rule of their conduct. They seem to look upon their offspring as merely slaves. They are fond of them in their way, no doubt, but the law of implicit obedience is maintained by dint of blows and stripes. The children are kicked, punched, and thrashed perpetually. A good ground-ash stick is the gospel of the labouring man. They carry the same plan into their work. How many carters have been severely fined and imprisoned for whipping, and sometimes even maiming, the boys under their commands? And yet the old practice still continues, only a little checked by wholesome terror of the law.

Despite of all the teaching of the Radical papers, all the whispers of the Methodist itinerant preachers, despite the hatred which the Labourers' Union agents endeavour to sow between the labourer and the farmer, still the great mass of labourers at the last election,★ wherever they had a vote, supported the local candidate—the man who represented the soil—and declined to do more than listen to the brilliant promises held out by the party of change. So strong above all things is the force of tradition and custom.

The agriculturists are firmly and earnestly wedded to that unwritten creed which has grown up among them out of the past. Why, then, should they be so hardly dealt with, more than others, for adhering to this faith? Argue with them, educate them up to your standard if you like—but is it fair, is it just, is it in accordance with that spirit of liberalism and tolerance which their opponents profess, to taunt, abuse, and bully to the full length that words will permit? They are not facile at expression, these same men of the soil. The flow of language seems denied to them. They are naturally a silent race—preferring deeds to speech. They live much with inarticulate nature. It may be, after all, they have learnt some useful and abiding lessons from that intercourse. The old shepherds on the plains of Chaldea, under the starry skies of the East, watched the motions of those shining bodies till they

★ Feb. 1874.

slowly built up a religion, which, mixed with much dross, nevertheless contained some truths which educated men profess to this hour. These English farmers also observe the changes of the seasons, and watch the face of heaven. Their deepest convictions are not to be lightly set aside. There are men amongst them of great powers of thought. I remember one at this moment whose grand old head would have been a study for an artist. A large head he had, well-balanced, broad and high at the forehead, deep-set eyes, straight nose, and firm chin—every outward sign of the giant brain within. But the man was dumb. The thoughts that came to him he could communicate roughly to his friends, but the pen failed him. The horny hand which results from manual labour is too stiff to wield the swiftly-gliding quill. But there is another species of hand-writing which is called Work—a handwriting which will endure when the scribblings of the hour are utterly forgotten. This writing he laboured at earnestly and eagerly, not for his own good either, for it absorbed his own fortune, no small one, in the attempt to realise his conception of machinery which would double the yield of food. It has been done since his time, other men stepping over the bridge of experience which he had built. Now this man, who, on the principles of the opponents of the agriculturists, was a benefactor to his species, and a pioneer of true progress, was, nevertheless, one of the firmest, staunchest, most uncompromising supporters of that creed which they are endeavouring to destroy, and which may be stated thus: 'I believe in the Sovereign, the Church, and the Land: the Sovereign being the father of the people in a temporal sense; the Church in a spiritual sense; and the Land being the only substantial and enduring means of subsistence. Cotton, coal, and iron cannot be eaten, but the land gives us corn and beef; therefore, the land stands first and foremost, and the agriculturist, as the tiller of land, possesses an inalienable right which it is his duty to maintain, and in so doing he is acting for the good of the community. I believe that the son and the daughter should obey their parents, and show regard to their wishes even when legally independent. Also that the servant should obey his employer. The connection between employer and employed does not cease with the payment of wages. It is the duty of the servant to show consideration for the advice of the master; and the master is not free from responsibility as to the education and the comfort of the man. The master is bound by all laws, human and divine, to pay a fair amount of wages for a day's work. If he does not do so he robs the workman as much as if he stole the money from his pocket. The workman is equally bound to do his work properly, and in neglecting to do so he robs his employer. To demand more wages than has been earned is an attempt at robbery. Both master and man should respect authority, and abide by its decisions.'

Such is a slight outline of the home-life and the faith of the farmer.

THE LABOURER'S DAILY LIFE

MANY labourers can trace their descent from farmers or well-to-do people, and it is not uncommon to find here and there a man who believes that he is entitled to a large property in Chancery, or elsewhere, as the heir. They are very fond of talking of these things, and naturally take a pride in feeling themselves a little superior in point of ancestry to the mass of labourers.

How this descent from a farmer to a labourer is managed there are at this moment living examples going about the country. I knew a man who for years made it the business of his life, to go round from farm to farm soliciting charity, and telling a pitiful tale of how he had once been a farmer himself. This tale was quite true, and as no class likes to see their order degraded, he got a great deal of relief from the agriculturists where he was known. He was said to have been wild in his youth, and now in his old age was become a living representative of the farmer reduced to a labourer.

This reduction is, however, usually a slow process, and takes two generations to effect—not two generations of thirty years each, but at least two successors in a farm.

Perhaps the decline of a farming family began in an accession of unwonted prosperity. The wheat or the wool went up to a high price, and the farmer happened to be fortunate and possessed a large quantity of those materials. Or he had a legacy left him, or in some way or other made money by good fortune rather than hard work. This elated his heart, and thinking to rise still higher in life, he took another, or perhaps two more large farms. But to stock these required more money than he could produce, and he had to borrow a thousand or so. Then the difficulty of attending to so large an acreage, much of it distant from his home, made it impossible to farm in the best and most profitable manner. By degrees the interest on the loan ate up all the profit on the new farms. Then he attempted to restore the balance by violent high farming. He bought manures to an unprecedented extent, invested in costly machinery—anything to produce a double crop. All this would have been very well if he had had time to wait till the grass grew; but meantime the steed starved. He had to relinquish the additional farms, and confine himself to the original one with a considerable loss both of money and prestige. He had no energy to rise again; he relapsed into slow, dawdling ways, perpetually regretting and dwelling on the past, yet making no effort to retrieve it.

This is a singular and strongly marked characteristic of the agricultural class, taken generally. They work and live and have their being in grooves. So long as they can continue in that groove, and go steadily forward, without much thought or trouble beyond that of patience and perseverance, all goes well; but if any sudden jolt should throw them out of this rut, they seem incapable of regaining it. They say, "I have lost my way; I shall never get it again." They sit down and regret the past, granting all their errors with the greatest candour; but the efforts they make to regain their position are feeble in the extreme.

So our typical unfortunate farmer folds his hands, and in

point of fact slumbers away the rest of his existence, content with the fireside and a roof over his head, and a jug of beer to drink. He does not know French, he has never heard of Metternich, but he puts the famous maxim in practice, and, satisfied with to-day, says in his heart, *Après nous le Déluge*. No one disturbs him; his landlord has a certain respect and pity for him—respect, perhaps, for an old family that has tilled his land for a century, but which he now sees is slowly but irretrievably passing away. So the decayed farmer dozes out his existence.

Meantime his sons are coming on, and it too often happens that the brief period of sunshine and prosperity has done its evil work with them too. They have imbibed ideas of gentility and desire for excitement utterly foreign to the quiet, peaceful life of an agriculturist. They have gambled on the turf and become involved. Notwithstanding, the fall of their father from his good position, they still retain the belief that in the end they shall find enough money to put all to rights; but when the end comes there is a deficiency. Among them there is perhaps one more plodding than the rest. He takes the farm, and keeps a house for the younger children. In ten years he becomes a bankrupt, and the family are scattered abroad upon the face of the earth. The plodding one becomes a bailiff, and lives respectably all his life; but his sons are never educated, and he saves no money; there is nothing for them but to go out to work as farm labourers.

Such is something like the usual way in which the decline and fall of a farming family takes place, though it may of course arise from unforeseen circumstances, quite out of the control of the agriculturist. In any case the children graduate downwards till they become labourers. Nowadays many of them emigrate, but in the long time that has gone before, when emigration was not so easy, many hundreds of families have thus become reduced to the level of labourers they once employed. So it is that many of the labourers of to-day bear names which less than two generations ago were well known and highly respected over a wide tract of country. It is natural for them to look back with a certain degree of pleasure upon that past, and some may even have been incited to attempt a return to the old position.

But the great majority, the mass, of the agricultural labourers have been labourers time out of mind. Their fathers were labourers, their grandfathers and their great-grandfathers have all worked upon the farms, and very often almost continuously during that long period of time upon the farms in one parish. All their relations have been, and still are, labourers, varied by one here who has become a tinker, or one there who keeps a small roadside beer-house. When this is the case, when a man and all his ancestors for generations have been hewers of wood and drawers of water, it naturally follows that the present representative of the family holds strongly to the traditions, the instincts, acquired during the slow process of time. What those instincts are will be better gathered from a faithful picture of his daily life.

Most of the agricultural labourers are born in a thatched cottage by the roadside, or in some narrow lane. This cottage is usually an encroachment. In the olden time, when land was cheap, and the competition for it dull, there were many strips and scraps which were never taken any notice of, and of which at this hour no record exists either in the parochial papers or the Imperial archives. Probably this arose from the character of the country in the past, when the greater part was open, or, as it was called, champaign land, without hedge, or ditch, or landmark. Near towns a certain portion was enclosed generally by the great landowners, or for the use of the tradesmen. There was also a large enclosure called the common land, on which all burgesses or citizens had a right to feed so many cattle, sheep, or horses. As a rule the common land was not enclosed by hedges in fields, though instances do occur in which it was. There were very few towns in the reign of Charles II. that had not got their commons attached to them; but outside and beyond these patches of cultivation round the towns the country was open, unenclosed, and the boundaries ill-defined. The king's highway ran from one point to another, but its course was very wide. Roads were not then macadamised and strictly confined to one line. The want of metalling, and the consequent fearful ruts and sloughs, drove vehicles and travellers further and further from what was the original line, till they formed a track perhaps a score or two of yards wide. When fields became more generally enclosed it was still only in patches, and these strips and spaces of green sward were left utterly uncared for and unnoticed. These were encamped upon by the gipsies and travelling folk, and their unmolested occupation no doubt suggested to the agricultural labourer that he might raise a cottage upon such places, or cultivate it for his garden.

I know of one spot at this present moment which was enclosed by an agricultural labourer fully sixty years ago. It is an oval piece of ground of considerable size, situated almost exactly in the centre of a very valuable estate. He and his descendants continued to crop this garden of theirs entirely unmolested for the whole of that time, paying no rent whatever. It soon, however, became necessary to enlarge the size of the fields, which were small, in order to meet the requirements of the modern style of agriculture. This oval piece was surrounded by hedges of enormous growth, and the cultivator was requested to remove to another piece more out of the way. He refused to do so, and when the proprietors of the surrounding estate came to inquire into the circumstances they found that they could do nothing. He had enjoyed undisturbed possession for sixty years; he had paid no rent—no quit rent or manor dues of any kind. But still further, when they came to examine the maps and old documents, no mention whatever appeared of this particular patch of ground. It was utterly unnoticed; it was not recorded as any man's property. The labourer therefore retained possession. This was an extraordinary case, because the encroachment took place in the middle of a cultivated estate, where one would have thought the tenants would have seen to it.

Commonly the squatters pitched on a piece of land—a long unused strip—running parallel to the highway or lane. This was no one's property; it was the property of the nation, which had no immediate representative to look after its interests. The surrounding farmers did not care to interfere; it was no business of theirs. The highway board, unless the instance was very glaring, and some actual obstruction of the road was caused, winked at the trespass. Most of them were farmers, and did not wish to interfere with a poor man, who they knew had no other way of getting a house of his own. By-and-by, when the cottage was built, the labourer was summoned to the court-leet of the manor, and was assessed in quit rent, a mere nominal sum, perhaps fourpence or a shilling a year. He had no objection to this, because it gave him a title. As long as the quit rent was duly paid, and he could produce the receipt, he was safe in the occupation of his cottage, and no one could turn him out. To be assessed by the court-leet in fact established his title. Some of these court-leets or manor courts are only held at intervals of three years, or even more, and are generally composed of farmers, presided over by the legal agent of the lord of the manor. The tenants of the manor attend to pay their quit rent for the preceding years, and it often happens that if the cottager has been ill, or is weak and infirm, the farmers composing the court subscribe and pay the quit rent for him.

The first step when a labourer intends to become a squatter is to enclose the strip of land which he has chosen. This he does by raising a low bank of earth round it, on which he plants elder bushes, as that shrub grows quickest, and in the course of two seasons will form a respectable fence. Then he makes a small sparred gate which he can fasten with a padlock, and the garden is complete. To build the cottage is quite another matter. That is an affair of the greatest importance, requiring some months of thought and preparation. The first thing is to get the materials. If it is a clay country, of course bricks must be chosen; but in stone countries there are often quarries on the farm on which he works. His employer will let him have a considerable quantity of stone for nothing, and the rest at a nominal charge, and will lend him a horse and cart at a leisure season; so that in a very short time he can transport enough stone for his purpose. If he has no such friend, there is almost sure to be in every parish a labouring man who keeps a wretched horse or two, fed on the grass by the roadside, and gains his living by hauling. Our architect engages this man at a low price to haul his materials for him. The lime to make mortar he must buy. In the parish there is nearly sure to be at least one native mason, who works for the farmers, putting up pig-styes, mending walls, and doing small jobs of that kind. This is the builder who engages to come on Saturday afternoons or in the evenings, while the would-be house-holder himself is the hod-bearer and mixes the mortar. Nine times out of ten the site for the cottage is chosen so as to have a ditch at the back. This ditch acts at once as the cesspool and the sewer, and, unless it happens to have a good fall, speedily becomes a nuisance to the neighbour-hood. A certain quantity of wood is of course required in building even this humble edifice. This is either given by the farmers or is purchased at a nominal rate.

The ground plan is extremely simple. It consists of two rooms, oblong, and generally of the same size—one to live in, the other to sleep in—for the great majority of the squatters' hovels have no upstair rooms. At one end there is a small shed for odds and ends. This shed used to be built with an oven, but now scarcely any labourers bake their own bread, but buy of the baker. The walls of the cottage having been carried up some six feet, or six feet six—just a little higher than a man's head—the next process is to construct the roof, which is a very simple process. The roof is then thatched, sometimes with flags cut from the brooks, but more usually with straw, and practically the cottage is now built, for there are no indoor fittings to speak of. The chimney is placed at the end of the room set apart for day use. There is no ceiling, nothing between the floor and the thatch and rafters, except perhaps at one end, where there is a kind of loft. The floor consists simply of the earth itself rammed down hard, or sometimes of rough pitching-stones, with large interstices between them. The furniture of this room is of the simplest description. A few chairs, a deal table, three or four shelves, and a cupboard, with a box or two in the corners, constitute the whole. The domestic utensils are equally few, and strictly utilitarian. A great pot, a kettle, a saucepan, a few plates, dishes and knives, half-a-dozen spoons, and that is about all. But on the mantelpiece there is nearly sure to be a few ornaments in crockery, bought from some itinerant trader. The walls are white-washed. The bedroom is plainly and rudely furnished. Some cottages do not even attain to this degree of comfort. They consist of four posts set in the ground which support the cross-beam and the roof, and the walls are made of wattle and daub, *i.e.*, of small split willow sticks, put upright and daubed over wth coarse plaster. The roofs of these cottages are often half hidden with rank grass, moss, and sillgreen, a vegetation perhaps encouraged by the drippings from a tree overhanging the roof; and the situation of the cottage is itself in many cases low and damp.

But there is a class of squatters, who possess habitations more fit for human beings. These were originally built by men who had saved a little money, had showed, perhaps, a certain talent for hedge carpentering or thatching, become tinkers, or even blacksmiths. In such capacities a man may save a little money—not much, perhaps £30 or £40 at furthest. With the aid of this he manages to build a very tidy cottage, in the face of the statement made by architects and builders that a good cottage cannot be erected under £120. Their dwellings do not, indeed, compete with the neat, prim, and business-like work of the professional builder; but still they are roomy and substantial cottages. The secret of cheapness lies in the fact that they work themselves at the erection, and do not entrust some one else with a contract. Moreover, they make shifts and put up with drawbacks as no business-man could possibly do. The materials they purchase are cheap and of second-class condition, but good enough to hold together and to last some time. Their rude beams and rafters would not satisfy the eye of a landed proprietor, but they hold up the roof-tree equally well. Every pound they spend goes its full length, and not a penny is wasted. After a while a substantial-looking cottage rises up, whitewashed and thatched. It has an upper storey with two rooms, and two, at least, downstairs, with the inevitable lean-to or shed, without which no labourer's cottage is complete. This is more like a house, the residence of a man, than that of the poorer squatter. The floor is composed of flagstones, in this case always carefully washed and holystoned. There are the same chairs and deal table as in the poorer cottage, but there are many more domestic utensils, and the chimney-piece is ornamented with more crockery figures. A few coarse prints hang against the walls. Some of these old prints are great curiosities in their way—hardly valuable enough for a collection, but very amusing. A favourite set of prints is the ride of Dick Turpin to York on Black Bess, representing every scene in that famous gallop. The upstair rooms are better furnished, and the beds often really good.

Some of these cottages in summer-time really approach something of that Arcadian beauty which is supposed to prevail in the country. Everything, of course, depends upon the character of the inmates. The dull tint of the thatch is relieved here and there by great patches of sill-green, which is religiously preserved as a good herb, though the exact ailments for which it is 'good' are often forgotten. One end of the cottage is often completely hidden with ivy, and woodbine grows in thickest profusion over the porch. Near the door there are almost always a few cabbage-rose trees, and under the windows grow wall-flowers and hollyhocks, sweet peas, columbine, and sometimes the graceful lilies of the valley. The garden stretches in a long strip from the door, one mass of green. It is enclosed by thick hedges, over which the dog-rose grows, and the wild convolvulus will blossom in the autumn. Trees fill up every available space and corner— apple trees, pear trees, damsons, plums, bullaces—all varieties. The cottagers seem to like to have at least one tree of every sort. These trees look very nice in the spring when the apple blossom is out, and again in the autumn when the fruit is ripe. Under the trees are gooseberry bushes, raspberries, and numbers of currants. The patches are divided into strips producing potatoes, cabbage, lettuce, onions, radishes, parsnips; in this kitchen produce, as with the fruit, they like to possess a few of all kinds. There is generally a great bunch of rhubarb. In odd corners there are sure to be a few specimens of southernwood, mugwort, and other herbs; not for use, but from adherence to the old customs. The 'old people' thought much of these 'yherbs,' so they must have some too, as well as a little mint and similar potherbs. In the windows you may see two or three geraniums, and over the porch a wicker cage, in which the "ousel cock, with orange-tawny bill," pours out his rich, melodious notes. There is hardly a cottage without its captive bird, or tame rabbit, or mongrel cur, which seems as much attached to his master as more highbred dogs to their owners.

These better cottages are extremely pleasing to look upon. There is an old English, homely look about them. I know a man now whose cottage is ornamented much in the way I have described, a man of sixty, who can neither read nor write, and is rude and uncouth in speech, yet everything about him seems pleasant and happy. To my eye the thatch and gables, and picturesque irregularity of this class of cottages, are more pleasing than the modern glaring red brick and prim slate of dwellings built to order, where everything is cut with a precise uniformity. If a man can be encouraged to build his own house, depend upon it it is better for him and his neighbours than that he should live in one which is not his own. The sense of ownership engenders a pride in the place, and all his better feelings are called into play. Some of these cottagers, living in such houses as these, are the very best labourers to be had. They stay on one farm a lifetime, and never leave it—an invaluable aid to a farmer. They frequently possess some little special knowledge of carpentering or blacksmith's work, which renders them extremely useful, and at the same time increases their earnings. These men are the real true peasantry, quiet and peaceful, yet strong and courageous. These are the class that should be encouraged by every possible means; a man who keeps his little habitation in the state I have described, who ornaments it within, and fills his garden with fruit and flowers, though he may be totally unable to read or to speak correctly, is nevertheless a good and useful citizen, and an addition to the stability of the State.

Though these cottages are worth the smallest sums comparatively, it is interesting to note with what pride and satisfaction the possessors contemplate leaving them to their children. Of course this very feeling, where there are quarrelsome relations, often leads to bickerings and strife. It is astonishing with what tenacity a man who thinks he has a claim to a part of such a small estate will cling to his cause, and will not hesitate to spend to maintain his claim all his little earnings on the third-class lawyers whom the agricultural poor mostly patronise. Even after every shadow of legal chance is gone, he still loudly declares his right; and there is more squabbling about the inheritance of these places than over the succession to great domains.

Another class of labourers' cottages is found chiefly in the villages. These were not originally erected for the purpose to which they are now applied; they were farmhouses in the days when small farms were the rule, or they were built for tradesmen who have long since departed. These buildings are divided into two, three, or more habitations, each with its family; and many makeshifts have to be resorted to to render them decent and comfortable. This class of cottage is to be avoided if possible, because the close and forced intercourse which must take place between the families generally leads to quarrels. Perhaps there is one pump for the entire building, and one wants to use it just at the moment that another requires water; or there is only one gateway to the court, and the passage is obstructed by the wheelbarrow of the other party. It is from these places that the greater part of the malcontents go up to the magistrates in petty sessions. It is rare, indeed, that the cottager living more or less isolated by the side of the road appears in a court of law. Of course, in these villages there are cottages which have been built expressly for the use of labouring men, and these, like those in the open country, may be divided into three classes—the hovel, the cottage proper, and the model modern cottage.

In the villages there is almost sure to be one or more cottages which carries one's idea of Lilliputian dwellings to the extreme. These are generally sheds or outhouses which have been converted into cottages. I entered one not long since which consisted of two rooms, one above and one below, and each of these rooms could not have measured, at a guess, more than six feet across. I had heard of this place, and expected to find it a perfect den of misery and wretchedness. No such thing. To my surprise the woman who opened the door was neatly clad, clean, and bright. The floor of the cottage was of ordinary flag-stones, but there was a ceiling whitewashed and clean. A good fire was burning in the grate—it was the middle of winter—and the room felt warm and comfortable. The walls were completely covered with engravings from the *Illustrated London News*. The furniture was equal to the furniture of the best cottages, and everything was ex-tremely clean. The woman said they were quite comfort-able; and although they could have had a larger cottage many times since, they never wished to change, as they had no children. That of course made a great difference. I never should have thought it possible for two human beings to have existed, much less been comfortable, in such a dimunitive place. Another cottage I know contains but one room altogether, which is about eight feet square; it is inhabited by a solitary old woman, and looks like a toy-house. One or two such places as these may be found in most villages, but it does not by any means follow that because they are small the inhabitants are badly off. The condition they are found in depends entirely upon the disposition of the inmates. If they are slatternly and dirty, the largest cottages would not improve them.

In some rural villages a great many cottages may be observed sadly out of repair—the thatch coming off and in holes, the windows broken, and other signs of dilapida-tion. This is usually set down to the landlord's fault, but if the circumstances are inquired into, it will often be found that the fault lies with the inmates themselves. These cottages are let to labourers at a merely nominal rent, and with them a large piece of allotment ground. But although they thus get a house and garden almost free, they refuse to do the slightest or simplest repairs. If the window gets broken—'Oh, let it stop; the landlord can do that.' If a piece of thatch comes off—'Oh, 'tisn't my house; let the landlord do it up.' So it goes on till the cottage is ready to tumble to pieces. What is the landlord to do? In his heart he would like to raze the whole village to the ground and rebuild it afresh. But there are not many who can afford such an expense. Then, if it were done, the old women and old men, and infirm persons who find a home in these places, would be driven forth. If the landlord puts up two hundred new cottages, he finds it absolutely necessary to get some kind of return for the capital invested. He does not want more than two and a half per cent.; but to ask that means a rise of perhaps a shilling a week. That is enough; the labourer seeks another tumbledown place where he can live for tenpence a week, and the poor and infirm have to go to the workhouse. So, rather than be annoyed with the endless complaints and troubles, to say nothing of the inevitable loss of money, the landlord allows things to go on as they are.

Among our English cottages in out-of-the-way places may be found curious materials for the study of character in humble life. In one cottage you may find an upright, stern-featured man, a great student of the Bible, and fond of using its language whenever opportunity offers, who is the representative of the old Puritan, though the denomination to which he may belong is technically known as the Methodist. He is stern, hard, uncompromising—one who sets duty above affection. His children are not spoiled because the rod is spared. He stands aloof from his fellows, and is never seen at the cottage alehouse, or lingering in groups at the cross-roads. He is certain to be at the 'anniversary,' *i.e.*, the commemoration of the foundation of the Methodist chapel of the parish. The very next cottage may contain the antithesis of this man. This is a genius in his way. He has some idea of art, as you may gather from the fanciful patches into which his garden is divided. He has a considerable talent for construction, and though he has never been an apprentice he can do something towards mending a cart or a door. He makes stands with wires to put flowers in for the farmers' parlours, and strings the dry oak-apples on wire, which he twists into baskets, to hold knicknackeries. He is witty, and has his jest for everybody. He can do something of everything—turn his hand any way—a perfect treasure on the farm. In the old days there was another character in most villages; this was the rhymer. He was commonly the fiddler too, and sang his own verses to tunes played by himself. Since the printing-press has come in, and flooded the country with cheap literature, this character has disappeared, though many of the verses these men made still linger in the countryside.

The ordinary adult farm labourer commonly rises at from four to five o'clock; if he is a milker, and has to walk some little distance to his work, even as early as half-past three. Four was the general rule, but of late years the hour has grown later. He milks till five or half-past, carries the yokes to the dairy, and draws water for the dairymaid, or perhaps chops up some wood for her fire to scald the milk. At six he goes to breakfast, which consists of a hunch of bread and cheese as a rule, with now and then a piece of bacon, and as a milker he receives his quart of beer. At breakfast there is no hurry for half-an-hour or so; but some time before seven he is on at the ordinary work of the day. If a milker and very early riser, he is not usually put at the heavy jobs, but allowances are made for the work he has already done. The other men on the farm arrive at six. At eleven, or half-past, comes luncheon, which lasts a full hour, often an hour and a quarter. About three o'clock the task of milking again commences; the buckets are got out with a good deal of rattling and noise, the yokes fitted to the shoulders, and away he goes for an hour or hour and a half of milking. That done, he has to clean up the court and help the dairymaid put the heavier articles in place; then another quart of beer, and away home. The time of leaving off work varies from half-past five to half-past six. At ordinary seasons the other men leave at six, but in haymaking or harvest time they are expected to remain till the job in hand that day is finished, often till eight or half-past. This is compensated for by a hearty supper and almost unlimited beer. The women employed in field labour generally leave at four, and hasten home to prepare the evening meal. The evening meal is the great event of the day. Like the independent gentleman in this one thing, the labourer dines late in the day. His midday meal, which is the farmer's dinner, is his luncheon. The labourer's dinner is taken at half-past six to seven in the evening, after he has got home, unlaced his heavy and cumbrous boots, combed his hair, and washed himself. His table is always well supplied with vegetables, potatoes, and particularly greens, of which he is peculiarly fond. The staple dish is, of course, a piece of bacon, and large quantities of bread are eaten. It is a common thing now, once or twice in the week, for a labourer to have a small joint of mutton, not a prime joint, of course, but still good and wholesome meat. Many of them live in a style, so far as eating and drinking is concerned, quite equal to the small farmers, and far superior to what these small farmers were used to. Instead of beer, the agricultural labourer frequently drinks tea with his dinner—weak tea in large quantities. After the more solid parts comes a salad of onions or lettuce. These men eat quantities which would half kill many townspeople. After dinner, if it is the season of the year, they go out to the allotment and do a little work for themselves, and then, unless the alehouse offers irresistible attractions, to bed. The genuine agricultural labourer goes early to bed. It is necessary for him, after the long toil of the day, on account of the hour at which he has to rise in the morning.

Men employed on arable farms, as carters, for instance, have to rise even earlier than dairymen. They often begin to bait their horses at half-past three, or rather they used to. This operation of baiting is a most serious and important one to the carter. On it depends the appearance of his team—with him a matter of honest and laudable ambition. If he wishes his horses to look fat and well, with smooth shiny coats, he must take the greatest care with their food, not to give them too much or too little, and to vary it properly. He must begin feeding a long time before his horses start to plough. It is, therefore, an object with him to get to rest early. In the winter time especially the labouring poor go to bed very soon, to save the expense of candles.

By the bye, the cottagers have a curious habit, which deserves to be recorded even for its singularity. When the good woman of the cottage goes out for half-an-hour to fetch a pail of water, or to gossip with a neighbour, she always leaves the door-key in the keyhole *outside*. The house is, in fact, at the mercy of any one who chooses to turn the key and enter. This practice of locking the door and leaving the key in it is very prevalent. The presence of the key is to intimate that the inmate has gone out, but will shortly return; and it is so understood by the neighbours. If a cottager goes out for the day, he or she locks the door, and takes the key with them; but if the key is left in the door, it is a sign that the cottager will be back in ten minutes or so.

The alehouse is the terrible bane of the labourer. If he can keep clear of that, he is clean, tidy, and respectable; but if he once falls into drinking habits, good-bye to all hopes of his rising in his occupation. Where he is born there will he remain, and his children after him.

Some of the cottagers who show a little talent for music combine under the leadership of the parish clerk and the patronage of the clergyman, and form a small brass band which parades the village at the head of the Oddfellows or other benefit club once a year. In the early summer, before the earnest work of harvest begins, and while the evenings begin to grow long, it is not unusual to see a number of the younger men at play at cricket in the meadow with the more active of the farmers. Most populous villages have their cricket club, which even the richest farmers do not disdain to join, and their sons stand at the wicket.

The summer is the labourer's good season. Then he can make money and enjoy himself. In the summer three or four men will often join together and leave their native parish for a ramble. They walk off perhaps some forty or fifty miles, take a job of mowing or harvesting, and after a change of scenery and associates, return in the later part of the autumn, full of the things they have seen, and eager to relate them to the groups at the cross-roads or the alehouse. The winter is under the best circumstances a hard time for the labourer. It is not altogether that coals are dear and firewood growing scarcer year by year, but every condition of his daily life has a harshness about it. In the summer the warm sunshine cast a glamour over the rude walls, the decaying thatch, and the ivy-covered window. The blue smoke rose up curling beside the tall elm-tree. The hedge parting his garden from the road was green and thick, the garden itself full of trees, and flowers of more or less beauty. Mud floors are not so bad in the summer; holes in the thatch do not matter so much; an ill-fitting window-sash gives no concern. But with the cold blasts and ceaseless rain of winter all this is changed. The hedge next the road is usually only elder, and this, once the leaves are off, is the thinnest, most miserable of shelters. The rain comes through the hole in the thatch (we are speaking of the large class of poor cottages), the mud floor is damp, and perhaps sticky. If the floor is of uneven stones, these grow damp and slimy. The cold wind comes through the ill-fitting sash, and drives with terrible force under the door. Very often the floor is one step lower than the ground outside, and consequently there is a constant tendency in rainy weather for the water to run or soak in. The elm-tree overhead, that appeared so picturesque in summer, is now a curse, for the great drops fall perpetually from it upon the thatch and on the pathway in front of the door. In great storms of wind it sways to and fro, causing no little alarm, and boughs are sometimes blown off it, and fall upon the roof-tree. The thatch of the cottage is saturated; the plants and grasses that almost always grow on it, and the moss, are vividly, rankly green; till all dripping, soaked, overgrown with weeds, the wretched place looks not unlike a dunghill. Inside, the draught is only one degree better than the smoke. These low chimneys, overshadowed with trees, smoke incessantly, and fill the room with smother. To avoid the draught, many of the cottages are fitted with wooden screens, which divide the room, small enough before, into two parts, the outer of which, towards the door, is a howling wilderness of draught and wet from under the door; and the inner part close, stuffy, and dim with smoke driven down the chimney by the shifting wind. Here the family are all huddled up together close over the embers. Here the cooking is done, such as it is. Here they sit in the dark, or in such light as is supplied by the carefully hoarded stock of fuel, till it is time to go to bed, and that is generally early enough. So rigid is the economy practised in many of these cottages that a candle is rarely if ever used. The light of the fire suffices, and they find their beds in the dark. Even when a labourer has risen in the scale, and has some small property, the enforced habits of early life cling to him; and I have frequently found men who were really worth some little money sitting at eight o'clock on a dark winter's night without a candle or lamp, their feet close to a few dying embers. The older people especially go to bed early. Going to some cottages once for a parish paper that had been circulated for signature, I rapped at the closed door. This was at half-past seven one evening in November. Again and again I hammered on the door; at last an old woman put her head out of window, and the following colloquy ensued:—

"What do'ee want?"

"The paper; have you signed it?'

"Lor, I doan't know. He's on the table—a bin ther ever since a come. Thee's can lift th' latch an' take 'un. *We bin gone to bed this two hours.*"

They must have gone upstairs at half-past five. To rise at five of a summer's morning, and see the azure of the sky and the glorious sun, may be, perhaps, no great hardship, although there are few persons who could long remain poetical on bread and cheese. But to rise at five on a dark winter's morning is a very different affair. To put on coarse nailed boots, weighing fully seven pounds, gaiters up above the knee, a short greatcoat of some heavy material, and to step out into the driving rain and trudge wearily over field after field of wet grass, with the furrows full of water; then to sit on a three-legged stool, with mud and manure half-way up the ankles, and milk cows with one's head leaning against their damp, smoking hides for two hours, with the rain coming steadily drip, drip, drip— this is a very different affair.

The 'fogger' on a snowy morning in the winter has to encounter about the most unpleasant circumstances imaginable. Icicles hang from the eaves of the rick, and its thatch is covered with snow. Up the slippery ladder in the dark morning, one knee out upon the snow-covered thatch, he plunges the broad hay-knife in and cuts away an enormous truss—then a great prong is stuck into this, a prong made on purpose, with extra thick and powerful handle, and the truss, well bound round with a horse-hair rope, is hoisted on the head and shoulders. This heavy weight the fogger has to carry perhaps half-a-mile through the snow; the furrows in the field are frozen over, but his weight crashes through the ice, slush into the chilly water. Rain, snow, or bitter frost, or still more bitter east winds—'harsh winds,' as he most truly calls them—the fogger must take no heed of either, for the cows must be fed.

A quart of threepenny ale for breakfast, with a hunch of bread and cheese, then out to work again in the weather, let it be what it may. The cowyards have to be cleaned out—if not done before breakfast—the manure thrown up into heaps, and the heaps wheeled outside. Or, perhaps, the master has given him a job of piece-work to fill up the middle of the day with—a hedge to cut and ditch. This means more slush, wet, cold, and discomfort. About six or half-past he reaches home, thoroughly saturated, worn-out, cross, and 'dummel.' I don't know how to spell that word, nor what its etymology may be, but it well expresses the dumb, sullen churlishness which such a life as this engenders. For all the conditions and circumstances of such a life tend to one end only—the blunting of all the finer feelings, the total erasure of sensitiveness. The coarse, half-cooked cabbage, the small bit of fat and rafty bacon, the dry bread and pint of weak tea, makes no very hearty supper after such a day as this. The man grows insensible to the weather, so cold and damp; his bodily frame becomes crusted over, case-hardened; and with this indifference there rises up at the same time a corresponding dulness as regards all moral and social matters.

Generally the best conditions of cottage life are to be found wherever there are, say, three or four great, tall, strong, unmarried sons lodging in the house with their aged parents. Each of these pays a small sum weekly for his lodging, and often an additional sum for the bare necessities of life. In the aggregate this mounts up to a considerable sum, and whatever is bought is equally shared by the parents. They live exceedingly well. Such young men as these earn good wages, and now and then make extra time, and come home with a pocketful of money. Even after the inevitable alehouse has claimed its share, there still remains enough to purchase fresh meat for supper; and it is not at all unusual in such cottages to find the whole family supping at seven (it is, in fact, dining) on a fairly good joint of mutton, with every species of common vegetables. In one case that was brought under my notice three brothers lived with their aged mother. They were all strong, hard-working men, and tolerably steady. In that cottage there were no less than four separate barrels of beer, and all on tap. Four barrels in one cottage seems an extraordinary thing, yet it resolved itself very simply. The cottage was the mother's; they gave her so much for lodging, and she had her own barrel of beer, so that there should be no dispute. The three brothers were mowers—mowers drink enormous quantities of liquor—and with the same view to prevent dispute each had his own especial barrel. Families like this live fairly well, and have many little comforts. Still, at the best, in winter it is a rough and uncomfortable existence.

In the life of the English agricultural labourers there is absolutely no poetry, no colour. Even their marriages—times when if ever in life poetry will manifest itself—are sober, dull, tame, clumsy, and colourless. I say sober in the sense of tint, for to get drunk appears to be the one social pleasure of the marriage-day. They, of course, walk to church; but then that walk usually leads across fields full of all the beauties of the spring or the summer. There is nothing in the walk itself to flatten down the occasion. But the procession is so dull—so utterly ungenial—a stranger might pass it without guessing that a wedding was toward. Except a few rude jests; except that there is an attempt to walk arm-in-arm (it is only an attempt, for they forget to allow for each other's motions); except the Sunday dresses, utterly devoid of taste, what is there to distinguish this day from the rest? There is the drunken carousal, it is true, all the afternoon and evening. There are no fête days in the foreign sense in the English labourer's life. There are the fairs and feasts, and a fair is the most melancholy of sights. Showmen's vans, with pictures outside of unknown monsters; merry-go-rounds, nut stalls, gingerbread stalls, cheap Jacks, and latterly photographic 'studios'; behind all these the alehouse; the beating of drums and the squalling of pigs, the blowing of horns, and the neighing of horses trotted out for show, the roar of a rude crowd—these constitute a country fair. There is no colour—nothing flowery or poetical about this festival of the labourer.

The village feasts are still less interesting. Here and there the clergyman of the parish has succeeded in turning what was a rude saturnalia into a decorous 'fête,' with tea in a tent. But generally the feasts are falling into rapid disuse, and would perhaps have died away altogether had not the benefit societies often chosen that day for their annual club-dinner. A village feast consists of two or three gipsies located on the greensward by the side of the road, and displaying ginger-beer, nuts, and toys for sale; an Aunt Sally; and, if the village is a large one, the day may be honoured by the presence of what is called a rifle-gallery; the 'feast' really and truly does not exist. Some two or three of the old-fashioned farmers have the traditional roast beef and plum-pudding on the day, and invite a few friends; but this custom is passing away. In what the agricultural labourer's feast nowadays consists no one can tell. It is an excuse for an extra quart or two of beer, that is all.

This dulness is not, perhaps, the fault of the labourer. It may be that it is the fault of the national character, shown more broadly in the lower class of the population. Speaking nationally, we have no fête days—there is no colour in our mode of life. These English agricultural labourers have no passion plays, no peasant plays, no rustic stage and drama, few songs, very little music. The club dinner is the real fête of the labourer; he gets plenty to eat and drink for that day. It is this lack of poetical feeling that makes the English peasantry so uninteresting a study. They have no appreciation of beauty. Many of them, it is true, grow quantities of flowers; but barely one in a thousand could arrange those flowers in a bouquet.

The alehouse forms no inconsiderable part of the labourer's life. It is at once his stock exchange, his reading-room, his club, and his assembly rooms. It is here that his benefit society holds its annual dinner. The club meetings take place weekly or monthly in the great room upstairs. Here he learns the news of the day; the local papers are always to be found at the public-house, and if he cannot read himself he hears the news from those who can. In the winter he finds heat and light, too often lacking at home; at all times he finds amusement; and who can blame him for seizing what little pleasure lies in his way? As a rule the beerhouse is the only place of amusement to which he can resort: it is his theatre, his music-hall, picture-gallery, and Crystal Palace. The recent enactments bearing upon the licensed victuallers have been rather hard upon the agricultural labourer. No doubt they are very excellent enactments, especially those relating to early closing; but in the villages and outlying rural districts, where life is reduced to its most rude and simple form, many of the restrictions are unjust, and deprive the labourer of what he feels to be his legitimate right. Playing at nine-pins, for instance, is practically forbidden, so also dominoes. Now, it was a great thing to put down skittle-sharping and cheating at gambling generally—a good thing to discourage gambling in every form—but in these thinly-populated outlying agricultural parishes, where money is scarce and wages low, there never existed any temptation

to allure skittle-sharpers and similar cheaters to the spot.
The game at skittles was a legitimate game—a fair and
honest struggle of skill and strength. Nine times out of ten
it was played only for a quart of ale, to be drunk by the
loser as well as the winner in good fellowship. Why deprive the man who labours all day in wet and storm of so
simple a pleasure in the evening? The conditions are very
different to those existing in large manufacturing towns,
and some modification of the law ought to be made. The
agricultural labourer has no cheap theatre at which he can
spend an hour, no music-hall, no reading-room; his only
resource is the public-house. Now that he is practically
deprived of his skittles and such games, he has no amusement left except to drink, or play at pitch and toss on the
quiet, a far worse pastime than skittles. Skittles, of course,
are allowed provided the players play for love only; but
what public-house keeper cares to put up the necessary
arrangements on such terms? The labourer will have his
quart in the evening, and, despite of all 'cry' to the contrary, I believe it to be his right to have that quart; and it is
better, if he must have it, that his whole thoughts should
not be concentrated on the liquor—that he should earn it
by skill and strength. There is an opprobrium about the
public-house, and let us grant that it is at least partially
deserved—but where else is the labourer to go? He cannot
for ever work all day and sit in his narrow cabin in the
evening. He cannot always read, and those of his class who
do read do so imperfectly. A reading-room has been tried,
but as a rule it fails to attract the *purely agricultural labourer*.
The shoemaker, the tailor, the village post-master, grocer,
and such people may use it; also a few of the better-
educated of the young labourers, the rising generation; but
not the full-grown labourer with a wife and family and

cottage. It does good undoubtedly; in the future, as education extends, it will become a place of resort. But at present it fails to reach the adult genuine agricultural labourer. For a short period in the dead of the winter the farmers and gentry get up penny readings in many places, but these are confined to at most one evening a week. What, then, is the labourer to do? Let any one put himself in his place, try to realise his feelings and circumstances. At present, till education extends, he must go to the public-house. Is he to be punished and deprived of his game of skill because in large towns it bears evil fruit? Surely the law could be somewhat modified, and playing permitted under some restrictions.

The early closing has been an unalloyed good in these rural districts. The labourer is a steady drinker. He does not toss down glasses of stiff brandy and whisky. His beer requires time to produce an effect. The last hour does the mischief. Since the earlier closing the village streets have been comparatively free from drunken men. In any case, the agricultural labourer is the most lamb-like of drunkards. He interferes with no one. He unhinges no gates, smashes no windows, does no injury. He either staggers home or quietly lies on the grass till the liquor passes off. He is not a quarrelsome man. He does not fight with knuckle-dusters or kick with his heavy boots. His fights, when he does fight, are very harmless affairs. No doubt his drunkenness is an offence; but it is comparatively innocuous to the general public.

Religious feeling does not run high among the labourers. A large proportion of them are Nonconformists—principally Methodists. But this is not out of any very decided notion as to the difference of ceremony or theological dogma; it arises out of a class feeling. They say, or rather they feel, that this is *their* church. The parish church is the church of the farmers and the gentry. There is no hostility to the clergyman of the parish, no bitter warfare of sect against sect, or of Methodist against Churchman. But you see very few of the farmers go to chapel. The labourer goes there, and finds his own friends—his cousins and uncles—his wife's relations. He is among his own class. There is no feeling of inferiority. The religion taught, the service, the hymns, the preacher, all are his. He has a sense of proprietorship in them. He helps to pay for them. The French peasant replied to the English tourist, who expressed surprise at the fanatic love of the populace for the first Napoleon—'he was as much a tyrant as King Louis was.' 'Ah, but Napoleon was *our* king.' So the labourers feel that this is their religion. Therefore it is that so many of them gather together (where there are no chapels) in the cottage of some man who takes the lead, and sit, with doors and windows shut, crammed together to pray and listen to others pray. Any of them who wishes can, as it were, ascend the pulpit here. This is why in so many parishes the pews of the parish church are comparatively empty so far as agricultural labourers are concerned. The best of clergymen must fail to fill them under such disadvantages.

It is very difficult not only for the clergyman, but for others who wish to improve the condition of the labourer, to reach him. Better cottages are, of course, a most effectual way, but it is not in the power of every one to confer so substantial a benefit. Perhaps one of the best means devised has been that of cottage flower-shows. These are, of course, not confined to flowers; in fact, the principal part of such shows consist of table vegetables and fruit. By rigidly excluding all gardeners, and all persons not strictly cottage people, the very best results have often been arrived at in this way. For if there is one thing in which the labourer takes an interest it is his garden and his allotment. To offer him prizes for the finest productions of his garden touches the most sensitive part of his moral organisation. It is wonderful what an amount of emulation these prizes excite—emulation not so much for the value of the prize as for the distinction. These competitions tend beside to provide him with a better class of food, for he depends largely upon vegetables.

There is nothing connected with the condition of the agricultural poor that is better worth the attention of improvers than the style of cookery pursued in these cottages. A more wretched cookery probably does not exist on the face of the earth. The soddened cabbage is typical of the whole thing. Since higher wages have come in it has become possible for the labourer in many cases to provide himself with better food, such as mutton—the cheap parts—more bacon, pork, and so on; but the women do not know how to make the most of it. It is very difficult to lay down a way in which this defect may be remedied; for there is nothing a man, let him be never so poor, so deeply resents as an inspection of the contents of his pot. He would sooner eat half-raw bacon than have the teaching forced on him—how to make savoury meals of the simple provisions within his reach; nor can he be blamed for this sturdy independent feeling. Possibly the establishment of schools of cookery in villages might do much good. They might be attached to the new schools now building throughout the country. The labourer, from so long living upon coarse, ill-cooked food, acquires an artificial taste. Some men eat their bacon raw; others will drink large quantities of vinegar, and well they may need it to correct by its acidity the effects of strong unwholesome cabbage. The cottage cook has no idea of those nutritious and pleasant soups which can be made to form so important a feature in the economy of daily life.

The labourer is in a lower degree of the same class as the third-rate working farmer of the past. He is the old small dairy farmer in a coarser shape. With a little less education, ruder manners, with the instincts of eating, drinking, and avarice more prominently displayed, he presents in his actual condition at this day a striking analogy to the agriculturist of a bygone time. In fact, those farmers of twenty or thirty acres, living in cottage-like homesteads, were barely distinguishable as far as *personnel* went from the labourers among whom they lived. This being the case, it is not surprising to find that the labourer of this day presents in general characteristics a marked affinity in ideas and sentiments to those entertained by the old farmer. He has the same paternal creed in a more primeval form. He considers his children as his absolute property. He rules them with a rod of iron, or rather of ground-ash. In fact, the ground-ash stick is his social religion. The agricultural labouring poor are very rough and even brutal towards their children. Not that they are without affection towards them, but they are used to thrash them into obedience instead of leading them into it by the gentle means of moral persuasion.

Bystanders would call the agricultural labourer cruel. Carters, for instance, had till lately a habit of knocking the boys under their control about in a brutal manner. But I do not think that in the mass of cases it arose from deliberate cruelty, but from a species of stolid indifference or insensibility to suffering. Somehow they do not seem to understand that others suffer, whether this arises from the rough life they lead, the endless battle with the weather, the hard fare—whether it has grown up out of the circumstances surrounding them. The same unfeeling brutality often extends to the cattle under their care. In this there has been a decided improvement of late years; but it is not yet extinct.

These are some of the lights and shades of the labourer's daily life impartially presented.

FIELD-FARING WOMEN

If a thoughtful English peasant-woman rejoiced that in her house a son was born, it would be, not because 'she had gotten a man from the Lord,' but a thanksgiving that it was not a girl. That most natural thanksgiving of the Hebrew woman is too rarely heard in the rural cottage, situated though it may be in the midst of meadows and fields abounding with the fat of the earth. The fact that a fresh being has entered upon life, with all its glorious possibilities, is not a subject for joy.

'Well, John,' the farmer says to his man, 'your wife has been confined, hasn't she? How's the young one?'

'Aw, sir, a' be main weak and pickèd, an' like *to go back*—thank God!' replies the labourer with intense satisfaction, especially if he has two or three children already. 'Pickèd' means thin, sharp-featured, wasted, emaciated. 'To go back' is to die. The man does not like to say 'die,' therefore he puts it 'to go back'—*i.e.*, whence it came; from the unknown. Yet, with all this hard indifference, the labourer is as fond of his children as any one else. The 'ego' that utters those apparently heartless words is not the real man, it is the 'ego' produced by long experience of the hardships of poverty; of coarse fare, rude labour, exposure. After all, it is in a spirit of tenderness towards the infant that the parent half desires it to die. The real 'ego,' the true man, delights as all humanity does in watching the growth of the tiny limbs, the expansion of the instincts into mind, and the first employment of that mind. He feels as Marguerite in *Faust* felt, tending the babe—'the holiest of all joys.' But life is very, very hard, and circumstances push him out of himself. Still more do these hardships tell upon his wife; and so it is, knowing what her sex have to go through, that she welcomes a boy more than a girl. An aged agricultural woman said she would sooner have seven boys than one girl; for the former, when they become lads, went out and earned their own living, but the girls you never knew when they were got rid of—they were always coming back. This expressed the practical view of the matter. But supposing that the child should prove a girl; it must not be imagined that it receives any ruder treatment in mere infancy than a boy would have had. In early infancy children have no sex. But the poor mother has her trials. Though in the midst of a country teeming with milk, it is often with the utmost difficulty that she can obtain any for her babe, if Nature shall have rendered her dependent upon artificial supply. This has become especially the case of late years, now that so much milk is sent to London, instead of being retained in the dairy for the manufacture of butter and cheese. So that it actually happens that the poor mother in the courts of the metropolis can obtain milk easier than her far-away sister in those fabulous fields which the city woman has never seen, and, perhaps, never will. Often in arable districts there are scarcely any cows kept. No one cares to retail a pennyworth of milk. It is only by favour, through the interest taken by some farmer's wife, that it can be got.

Very few agricultural women have a medical man present at their confinement; they usually entrust themselves to the care of some village nurse, who has a reputation for skill in such matters, but no scientifically acquired knowledge—who proceeds by rule of thumb. The doctor—almost always the parish doctor, though sometimes the club officer—is not called in till after the delivery. The poor woman will frequently come downstairs on the fourth day; and it is to this disregard of proper precautions that the distortions of figure and many of the illnesses of poor agricultural women are attributable. Nothing but the severe training they have gone through from childhood upwards—the exposure to all kinds of weather—the life in the open air, the physical strength induced by labour, can enable them to support the strain upon the frame caused by so quickly endeavouring to resume their household duties. It is probably this reserve of strength which enables them to recover from so serious a matter so quickly. Certain it is that very few die from confinement; and yet, from the point of view of the middle class of society, almost every precaution and every luxury by them deemed necessary is omitted. Of course, in some instances, agricultural women whose husbands have, perhaps, worked for one master from boyhood, receive much more attention than here indicated—wines, jellies, meat, and so on—but the majority have to rely upon the tender mercies of the parish. It has been often remarked that the labourer, let him be in receipt of what wages he will, makes no provision for this, the most serious and interesting of all domestic events. Though it can be foreseen for months, he does not save a single sovereign. He does not consider it in the least shameful to receive parish relief on these occasions; he leaves his partner entirely to the mercy of strangers, and were it not for the clergyman's wife, she would frequently be without sympathy. There are no matters in which so much practical good is accomplished by the wives of the rural clergy as in these confinements of the poor women in their parishes. It is a matter peculiarly within their sphere, and, to their honour be it spoken, one which they carry out to the utmost of their ability.

A cottage is at best a wretched place to be ill in. It is a marvel how many poor women escape at all. From the close atmosphere of the low-pitched holes in which they are confined. It is a wonder that, among the many schemes of philanthropy which have attracted attention of late years, something has not been done for these poor creatures. Why should not every large village or cluster of villages—there are often three or four within a mile or two—have their lying-in hospitals, on the cottage hospital system? Scarcely any parish but has its so-called charities—money left by misguided but benevolent persons, for the purpose of annual distribution in small doles of groats, or loaves, or blankets. Often there is a piece of land called 'Poor's Mead,' or some similar name, which has been devised like this, the annual rent from it to be applied for the poor. As it is, the benefit from these charities is problematical. If they were combined, and the aggregate funds applied to maintain a lying-in hospital for the district, a real and efficient good would be arrived at. But of all places, villages are neglected. Let it be drainage, water supply, allotments—anything and everything—the villages go on as they may, the fault being the absence of local authority. There are plenty of gentlemen ready and willing to take part in and advance such schemes, but there is no combination. Spontaneous combination is uncertain in its operation. If there were some system of village self-government, these wants would be soon supplied. It is true that there is the Union Workhouse. A poor woman can go to the workhouse; but is it right, is it desirable from any point of view, that decent women should be driven to the workhouse at such times? As a matter of fact, it is only the unfortunates who have illegitimate children that use the workhouse lying-in wards. Such an institution as has been suggested would be gladly welcomed by the agricultural poor. Most cottages have but two bedrooms, some only one; a better class of cottage is now being gradually erected with three, but even in these the third is very small. Now, take the case of a labouring man with seven or eight children, and living in a cottage with two bedrooms, and whose wife is confined; and let it be remembered that large families are common amongst this class. The wife must certainly have one room to herself and her attendant. The father, then, and his children must crowd into the other, or sleep as they can on the ground-floor. In the case of nearly grown-up children the overcrowding is a serious matter. The relief afforded by a lying-in hospital would be immense; and the poor woman herself would be restored to her family with her health firmly re-established, whereas now she often lingers in a sickly state for months.

In the soft, warm summer-time, when the midsummer hum of the myriads of insects in the air sheds a drowsy harmony over the tree-tops, the field-faring woman goes out to haymaking, and leaves her baby in the shade by the hedge-side. A wooden sheepcage, turned upside down and filled with new-made hay, forms not at all a despicable cradle; and here the little thing lies on its back and inhales the fresh pure air, and feels the warmth of the genial sun, cheered from time to time by visits from its busy mother. Perhaps this is the only true poetry of the hayfield, so much talked of and praised. The mother works with her rake, or with a shorter, smaller prong; and if it is a large farm, the women are kept as much as possible together, for their strength and skill will not allow them to work at the same pace as the men, and if they work in company the one hinders the other. A man can do the work of two women, and do it better in every way, besides being capable of the heavier tasks of pitching, cock-making, &c., which the women cannot manage. Before the haymaking machines and horse-rakes came into vogue, it was not uncommon to see as many as twenty women following each other in *échelon*, turning a 'wallow,' or shaking up the green swathes left by the mowers. Farmers were obliged to employ them, but were never satisfied with their work, which was the dearest they paid for. Somehow, there was no finish to it. Large numbers of women still work in the hayfield, but they are not used in gangs so much as formerly, but distributed about to do light jobs for which a man cannot be spared, and in these they are useful. The pay used to be tenpence a day; now it is one shilling and a pint of beer per day, and in some places fifteenpence. The Arcadian innocence of the hayfield, sung by the poets, is the most barefaced fiction; for those times are the rural saturnalia, and the broadest and coarsest of jokes and insinuations are freely circulated; nor does it always stop at language only, provided the master be out of sight. Matrons and young girls alike come in for an equal share of this rude treatment, and are quite a match for the men in the force of compliment. The women leave work an hour or so before the men, except when there is a press, and the farmer is anxious to get in the hay before a storm comes. It is not that the hayfield itself originates this coarseness, but this is almost the only time of the year when the labouring classes work together in large numbers. A great deal of farm-work is comparatively solitary; in harvest droves of people are collected together, and the inherent vulgarity comes out more strongly. At the wheat-harvest the women go reaping, and exceedingly hard they work at it. There is no harder work done under the sun than reaping, if it is well followed up. From earliest dawn to latest night they swing the sickles, staying with their husbands, and brothers, and friends, till the moon silvers the yellow corn. The reason is because reaping is piece-work, and not paid by the day, so that the longer and the harder they work the more money is earned. In this a man's whole family can assist. His wife, his grown-up sons and daughters cut the corn, the younger ones can carry it and aid in various ways.

It is wonderful how the men stand the excessive and continuous labour; it is still more wonderful how the women endure it, trying as it is to the back. It is the hottest season of the year—the early autumn; the sun burns and scorches, and the warm wind gives no relief; even the evenings are close and sultry. The heated earth reflects the rays, and the straw is dry and warm to the touch. The standing corn, nearly as high as the reaper, keeps off the breeze, if there is any, from her brow. Grasping the straw continuously cuts and wounds the hand, and even gloves will hardly give perfect protection. The woman's bare neck is turned to the colour of tan; her thin muscular arms bronze right up to the shoulder. Short time is allowed for refreshment; right through the hottest part of the day they labour. It is remarkable that none, or very few, cases of sunstroke occur. Cases of vertigo and vomiting are frequent, but pass off in a few hours. Large quantities of liquor are taken to sustain the frame weakened by perspiration.

When night does arrive, even then the task is not over, for they have to carry home on their heads the bundle of wheat gleaned by the smaller children, and perhaps walk two miles to the cottage. This is indeed work for a woman still suckling her child. It is not easy to calculate what a woman earns at such seasons, because they rarely work on their own account: either the father or the husband receives the wages in a lump with his own; but it cannot be much less than that earned by a man; for at these times they work with a will, and they do not at the haymaking. While reaping the baby is nestled down on a heap of coats or shawls under the shelter of the shocks of corn, which form a little hut for it, and, as in the hayfield, is watched by one of the children. Often three or four women will place their babies close together, and leave one great girl in charge of the whole, which is an economy, releasing other children for work; for the hayfield and the corn-harvest are the labourer's gold-mine. There is not so much rough joking in the corn-field; they do not work so close together, and the husband or father is near at hand; neither is there time nor inclination in the midst of such severe labour, to which haymaking is play.

Harvest-homes are going out of fashion. After one of these feasts there was often much that was objectionable; and, wherever possible, farmers have abolished them, giving a small sum of money instead; but in places the labourers grumble greatly at the change, preferring the bacon and the beer, and the unrestrained license. It is noticeable how the women must have their tea. If it is far from home, the children collect sticks, and a fire is made in a corner of the field, and the kettle boiled; and about four o'clock they take a cup in company—always weak tea, with a little brown sugar and no milk, and usually small pieces of bread sopped in it, especially by the elder women. Tea is largely used by the agricultural labourers, though it does not by any means prevent them from indulging in beer. Snuff is not taken by the women half so much as formerly, though some of the old ones are very fond of it.

As soon as ever the child is old enough to crawl about, it is sure to get out into the road and roll in the dust. It is a curious fact that the agricultural children, with every advantage of green fields and wide open downs, always choose the dusty hard road to play in. They are free to wander as they list over mead and leaze, and pluck the flowers out of the hedges, and idle by the brooks, all the year round, the latter part of the spring, when the grass is nearly fit for mowing, only excepted. Yet, excepting a few of the older boys birdnesting, it is the rarest thing to meet a troop of children in the fields; but there they are in the road, the younger ones sprawling in the dust, their naked limbs kicking up clouds, and the bigger boys clambering about in the hedge-mound bounding the road, making gaps, splashing in the dirty water of the ditches. Hardy young dogs one and all. Their food is of the rudest and scantiest, chiefly weak tea, without milk, sweetened with moist sugar, and hunches of dry bread, sometimes with a little lard, or, for a treat, with treacle. Butter is scarcely ever used in the agricultural labourer's cottage. It is too dear by far, and if he does buy fats, he believes in the fats expressed from meats, and prefers lard or dripping. Children are frequently fed with bread and cheap sugar spread on it. This is much cheaper than butter. Sometimes they get a bit of cheese or bacon, but not often, and a good deal of strong cabbage, soddened with pot-liquor. The elder boys get a little beer; the young girls none, save perhaps a sip from their mother's pint, in summer. This is what they have to build up a frame on capable of sustaining heat and cold, exposure, and a life of endless labour. The boys it seems to suit, for they are generally tolerably plump, though always very short for their age. Frequently teams of powerful horses drawing immense loads of hay or straw may be seen on the highway, in the charge of a boy who does not look ten years old judged by the town standard, but who is really fifteen. These short, broad, stout lads, look able to stand anything, and in point of fact do stand it, from the kick of a carter's heavy boot to the long and bitter winter. If it is wished to breed up a race of men literally 'hard as nails,' no better process could be devised; but, looked at from a mental and moral point of view, there may be a difference of opinion.

The girls do not appear to thrive so well upon this dietary. They are as tall as the boys, taller if anything considering the ages, but thin and skinny, angular and bony. At seven or eight years old the girl's labour begins. Before that she has been set to mind the baby, or watch the pot, and to scour about the hedges for sticks for the fire. Now she has not only to mind the baby, but to nurse it; she carries it about with her in her arms; and really the infant looks almost as large as herself, and its weight compels her to lean backwards. She is left at home all day in charge of the baby, the younger children, and the cottage. Perhaps a little bread is left for them to eat, but they get nothing more till the mother returns about half-past four, when, woe be to the girl if the fire is not lit, and the kettle on. The girl has to fetch the water—often a hard and tedious task, for many villages have a most imperfect supply, and you may see the ditches by the roadside dammed up to yield a little dirty water. She may have to walk half-a-mile to the brook, and then carry the bucket home as best she may, and repeat the operation till sufficient has been acquired; and when her mother is washing or, still worse, is a washerwoman by profession, this is her weary trudge all day. Of course there are villages where water is at hand, and sometimes too much of it. I know a large village where the brook runs beside the highway, and you have to pass over a 'drock,' or small bridge, to get to each of the cottages; but such instances are rare. The girl has also to walk into the adjacent town and bring back the bread, particularly if her mother happens to be receiving parish pay. A little older—at ten or eleven, or twelve—still more skinny and bony now as a rule, she follows her mother to the fields, and learns to pick up stones from the young mowing grass, and place them in heaps to be carted away to mend drinking places for cattle. She learns to beat clots and spread them with a small prong; she works in the hayfield, and gleans at the corn-harvest. Gleaning— poetical gleaning—is the most unpleasant and uncomfortable of labour, tedious, slow, backaching work; picking up ear by ear the dropped wheat, searching among the prickly stubble.

Notwithstanding all her labour, and the hardship she has to endure—coarse fare, and churlish treatment at the hands of those who should love her most—the little agricultural girl still retains some of that natural inclination towards the pretty and romantic inherent in the sex. In the spring she makes daisy chains, and winds them round the baby's neck; or with the stalks of the dandelion makes a chain several feet in length. She plucks great bunches of the beautiful bluebell, and of the purple orchis of the meadow; gathers heaps of the cowslip, and after playing with them a little while, they are left to wither in the dust by the roadside, while she is sent two or three miles with her father's dinner. She chants snatches of rural songs, and sometimes three or four together, joining hands, dance slowly round and round, singing slowly rude rhymes describing marriage—and not over decent some of these rhymes are. She has no toys—not one in twenty such girls ever have a doll; or, if they do, it is but some stick dressed in a rag. Poor things! they need no artificial dolls; so soon as ever they can lift it, they are trusted with the real baby. Her parents probably do not mean to be unkind, and use makes this treatment bearable, but to an outsider it seems unnecessarily rough, and even brutal. Her mother shouts at her in a shrill treble perpetually; her father enforces his orders with a harsh oath and a slap.

The pressure of hard circumstances, the endless battle with poverty, render men and women both callous to others' feelings, and particularly strict to those over whom they possess unlimited authority. But the labourer must not be judged too harshly: there is a scale in these matters; a proportion as in everything else; an oath from him, and even a slap on the ear, is really the counterpart of the frown and emphasised words of a father in a more fortunate class of life; and the children do not feel it, or think it exceptionally cruel, as the children of a richer man would. Undoubtedly, however, it does lessen the bond between child and parent. There is little filial affection among these cottagers—how should there be? The boy is driven away from home as early as possible; the girl is made day by day to feel her fault in being a girl; to neither can the poor man give any small present, or any occasional treat. What love there is lasts longest between the mother and her daughter. The only way in which a labourer exhibits his affection is when another labourer in authority, as a carter, ill-treats his boy—a too common case—and then he speaks loudly, and very properly. But even in most serious matters there is a strange callousness. I have known instances in which a father, aware that a criminal assault has been attempted by another labourer upon a tender child of twelve, has refused to prosecute, and the brutal offender would have escaped without the slightest punishment had not the clergyman heard of the story.

The slow years roll by—they are indeed slow in an agricultural village—and the girl, now fifteen, has to go regularly to work in the fields; that is, if the family be not meantime largely increased. She has in this latter case plenty of work at home to assist her mother. Cottagers are not over-clean, but they are not wilfully dirty in their houses; and with a large family there is much washing and other domestic matters to attend to, which the mother, now fast growing feeble, cannot get through herself. In harvest the women get up at four or earlier, and do their household work before starting for the fields. But, perhaps, by this time another girl has grown up sufficiently to nurse baby, mind the young ones, and do slave's work generally. Then the elder daughter goes to the fields daily when there is work to be had. In arable districts the women do much work, picking couch grass—a tedious operation—and hoeing. They never or rarely milk now. In the dead of winter there is nothing for women to do. At this age—fifteen or sixteen—the girl perhaps goes out to service at some farmhouse. If she is fortunate enough to enter the house of one of the modern class of farmers, it is a lucky day for her when she begins indoor labour. It is to be feared that the life of a girl of this kind in the old time, and not so long ago, in the houses of the poorer order of farmers, was a rough one indeed. But much of that is past, never to return, and our business is with the present. Where they have a dairy she has to clean the buckets and milk-cans and other utensils, to help turn the cheeses, and assist the dairymaid (a most important personage this last) in all kinds of ways. The work is coarse and rude, but it only lasts a portion of the day, and she has regular and ample meals. The bacon and cheese soon begin to tell upon her. The angular bones disappear, the skinny arms grow round, and presently enormously fat—not much the prettier, perhaps, but far more pleasant to look at. Her face loses the pinched expression; her cheeks become full, and round, and rosy; in every way her physical frame improves. It is wonderful what a difference a few months in a good farmhouse makes to a girl of this kind. She soon begins to dress better, not from her wages, for these are small enough, and may commence as low as £4; but her mistress gives her many things, and, if she is a good girl, buys her a dress now and then; and with the shilling or two she asks in advance, she purchases cheap ornaments of the pedlar at the door. Her life is low enough socially—it is almost an annual round of working, eating, and sleeping (no one sleeps like a farmwench); but it is an infinite improvement upon the struggle for existence at the cottage. She has no trouble, no thought, no care now. Her mistress may snap occasionally, her master may grumble, and the dairymaid may snarl; but there are no slaps on the ear, no kicks, no going to bed supperless. In summer she goes out in the afternoon haymaking as an extra hand, but only works a few hours, and it is really only a relaxation. She picks up some knowledge of cooking, learns how to make herself useful in the house, and in the course of a year or two, if moderately sharp, is capable of rising a degree, and obtaining a better salary as a maid-servant, having nothing to do with a dairy. The four or five pounds with which she commences may seem a very low sum, but the state of her domestic education at the time must be taken into consideration. She has to learn everything. All the years spent in working in the cottage at home have to be relearnt—all the old habits replaced by new ones. After the first year or so her value rises considerably; she may continue in the house at a higher salary, or go into the town as maid-servant in a tradesman's family. A large proportion of servant-girls thus find their way from the country into the town. With these we have nothing further to do—they are no longer field-farers. A few after several years learn the art and mystery of butter and cheese, and become dairymaids; and then, if they are clever, earn good wages—indeed, fabulous prices are asked by them. There are not, however, so many dairymaids as formerly, for the small dairies are getting amalgamated and made into larger ones, and then the farmer, if he makes butter and cheese, employs a dairyman in preference. This rise to be maid-servant, or to be dairy-maid, is the bright side of the girl's career. There are darker shades which must be mentioned.

The overcrowding in cottages leads to what may be called an indifference to decency. It is not that in families decency is wantonly and of a set purpose disregarded, but stern necessity leads to a coarseness and indelicacy which hardens the mind and deadens the natural modesty of even the best girls. Then the low scandals of the village talked over from cottage to cottage, the rude jokes of the hayfield, the general looseness and indifference which prevail as to morality, all prepare the girl for the too common fall. If she remains at home and works in the fields after the age of fifteen, unless uncommonly strong-minded, it is an open question whether she will or will not succumb. If she goes into a farmhouse as servant, the chances are in favour of her escaping temptation. But in farmhouses she may also sometimes run into the very jaws of danger. It is not uncommon in some districts for young labourers to sleep in the house, one or two who milk and have to be on the spot early. These take their supper in the kitchen or the brewhouse, and, despite the strictest precautions on the part of the mistress, enjoy plenty of opportunities for flirting with the girl. Young, full of animal spirits, giddy and ignorant, she thinks no harm of a romp, and finally falls, and has to leave her service. If a little may be said in favour of the poor girls, not a word can be said in favour of the agricultural men, who are immoral almost without exception, and will remain so until a better-educated generation with more self-respect arises. The number of poor girls, from fifteen to five-and-twenty, in agricultural parishes who have illegitimate offspring is extremely large, and is illustrated by the fact that, out of the marriages that take place—and agricultural poor are a marrying class—scarcely any occur until the condition of the girl is too manifest to be any longer concealed. Instances could be mentioned where the clergyman's wife, with a view to check the immorality around her, has offered a reward of a piece of furniture to the first married woman who does not bear a child till nine months after marriage; the custom being within three months. The frequency of the appeals to the petty sessions in rural districts for orders of contribution, by young unmarried girls, also illustrates the prevalent immorality. Of late the magistrates have taken the line of ordering contributions on a higher scale, on the grounds that the labourer earns larger wages, and that the cost of living has risen, and also as a check upon the men.

This well-intentioned step has had the precisely opposite effect to what was wished. The labourer with higher wages feels the demand upon his pocket but very little more. The cost of living in rural outlying districts has risen only to a very trifling degree—barely perceptibly, in fact. Bread is cheap—that is the staple—rents are the same, and there are more allotments than ever, making vegetables more easy to obtain. The result, therefore, is this, that the girl feels she can sin with comparative immunity. She is almost sure to get her order (very few such appeals are refused); let this be supplemented with some aid from the parish, and she is none the worse off than before, for there is no prejudice against employing her in the fields. Should her fall take place with some young farmer's son from whom she may get a larger contribution in private, or by order of the magistrates, she is really and truly in a pecuniary sense better off than she was before, for she has a certain fixed income. The evil is aggravated by the new law, which enables the order to be extended over a longer term of years than formerly, so that for fifteen years is a common thing. If it is decided to recognise immorality, and to provide against the woman being unduly injured by it, then these orders are certainly the correct procedure; but if it is desired to suppress it, then they are a total failure. The girl who has had an illegitimate child is thought very little the worse of by her friends and her own class, especially if her seducer is a man who can afford to pay for it—that is the grand point. If she is fool enough to yield to a man who is badly off, she may be jeered at as a fool, but rarely reprimanded as a sinner, not even by her own mother. Such things are not looked upon by the rural poor as sins, but as accidents of their condition.

It is easy to be hard upon the poor girls, but consider

their training. Many of them cannot read or write; how many even can sew well? The cottage girl is always a poor hand at her needle, and has to be taught by the elder servants when she first goes into her place. Accustomed from childhood to what would be considered abominable indecency in a higher class of life; constantly hearing phrases which it is impossible to allude to; running wild about the lanes and fields with stalwart young men coarser and ruder than those at home; seeing other girls none the worse off, and commiserated with rather than condemned, what wonder is it if the natural result takes place? The fairs have been credited with much of the mischief, and undoubtedly they are productive of evil; but if they were abolished, the average would in all probability remain about the same. The evil is inherent, and does not depend upon circumstances. It is the outcome of a long series of generations; it cannot be overcome in a decade. Education will do much, but not all. Youth is always led by the tone of the elder people. Until the tone of the parent is improved, the conduct of the young will remain much the same. The more distant a parish from a town, the more outlying and strictly agricultural, and therefore stagnant, the greater the immorality. It is the one blot upon the character of the agricultural poor. They are not thieves, they are not drunkards; if they do drink they are harmless, and it evaporates in shouting and slang. They are not riotous; but the immorality cannot be gainsaid. No specific cure for this state of things can be devised: it must slowly work itself out under the gradual pressure of an advancing social state. It will be slow; for, up to the present, the woman has had but a small share of the benefit that has befallen the labourer through higher wages. If higher wages mainly go for drink, the wife at home is not much the better. The women say themselves they are no better off.

If the girl at eighteen or twenty—in most agricultural marriages the girls are very young—is fortunate enough to have placed her faith in a man who redeems his word, then comes the difficulty of the cottage and the furniture to fill it. Cottages are often difficult to find, especially anywhere near a man's work, which is the great object. The furniture required is not much, but there must be some. The labourer does not deal much with the town furniture-dealer. A great deal of the furniture in cottages has been picked up at the sales of farmers on quitting their tenancies. Such are the old chairs, the formal sideboards and eight-day clocks standing in tall, square oaken cases by the staircase in the cottage. Such, too, are the great wooden bedsteads of oak or maple upstairs; and from the same source come the really good feather-beds and blankets. The women—especially the elder women—go to great trouble, and pinch themselves, to find a way of purchasing a good bed, and set no small pride upon it. These old oaken bedsteads, and sideboards, and chairs have perhaps been in the farmhouse for three or four generations, and are at last sold because the final representative of the family is imbued with modern ideas, and quits farming for trade. The cottagers always attend sales like this, and occasionally get hold of good bargains, and so it is that really good substantial furniture may often be found in the possession of the better class of labourers. The old people accumulate these things, and when their sons or daughters marry, can generally spare a few chairs, a bedstead and bed, and with a little crockery from other relations, and a few utensils bought in the adjacent town, the cottage is furnished sufficiently well for a couple whose habits are necessarily simple. After marriage the hard work of the woman's life really begins—work compared with which her early experience at home is nothing; and many, if they have left situations in farmhouses, deeply regret the change. The labourer can hardly be expected to feel the more exalted sentiments; and if in the upper classes even it is said that romance ends with marriage, it is doubly, literally true of the agricultural poor. In addition to her household work, she has to labour in the fields, or to wash—perhaps worse than the former alternative; and after a while her husband, too commonly wearying of his home, in which he finds nothing but a tired woman and troublesome children, leaves her for the public-house, and consumes two-thirds of their slender income in beer. The attachment of the woman for her husband lasts longer than that of the man for the woman. Even when he has become a confirmed drunkard, and her life with incessant labour has become a burden to her, she will struggle on, striving to get bread for the children and the rent for the landlord. She knows that as evening comes on, instead of sitting down to rest, her duty will be to go down to the public-house and wait till it pleases her lord and master to try to stagger home, and then to guide his clumsy steps to the threshold. Of course there are wives who become as bad as their husbands, who drink, or do worse, and neglect their homes, but they are the exception. As a rule, the woman, once married, does her best to keep her home together.

The wife of the labourer does not get her shins smashed with heavy kicks from hobnailed boots, such as the Lancashire ruffians administer; but, although serious wife-beating cases are infrequent, there are few women who escape an occasional blow from their husbands. Most of them get a moderate amount of thrashing in the course of their lives, and take it much as they take the hardships and poverty of their condition, as a necessity not to be escaped. The labourer is not downright brutal to his wife, but he certainly thinks he has a right to chastise her when she displeases him. Once in authority, the labourer is stern, hard, and inconsiderate of the feelings of others, and he is in authority in his own cottage. The wife has been accustomed to such treatment more or less from her childhood; she has been slapped and banged about at home, and therefore, thinks comparatively little of a blow from her husband's hand. The man does not mean it so brutally as it appears to outsiders. This semi-wife-beating is only too prevalent.

Does the incessant labour undergone by an agricultural woman result in ill effects to her physical frame? The day-work in the fields, the haymaking, and such labour as is paid for by the day and not by the piece, cannot do any injury, for it is light, and the hours are short. In some districts the women do not come before half-past eight, and leave a little after four, and they have a long hour out for dinner. It is the piece-work of the corn-harvest that tries the frame, when work begins at sunrise or shortly after, and lasts till the latest twilight, and when it is work, real muscular strain. This cannot but leave its mark. Otherwise the field is not injurious to the woman so far as the labour is concerned and the exposure is not so great as has been supposed, because women are scarcely ever expected to work in wet weather. The worst of the exposure is probably endured upon the arable fields in the bitter winds of spring; but this does not last very long. In what way field-labour is degrading to the women it is difficult to understand. The only work of a disgusting nature now performed by women is the beating of clots on pastureland, and that is quickly over. After all, there is nothing so very dreadful in it. Stone-picking, couch-clearing, hoeing, hay-making, reaping, certainly none of these are in any way disgusting operations. Women do not attend to cattle now. As to the immorality, undoubtedly a great deal of what is coarse and rude does pass upon the hayfield, but the hayfield does not originate it; if the same men and women met elsewhere, the same jokes would be uttered and conduct indulged in. The position of agricultural women is a painful one to contemplate, and their lives full of hardships; but field-labour cannot be fairly accused as the cause of the evils they endure. Their strength is overstrained in the cornfield; but what can you do? It is their gold-mine—their one grand opportunity of getting a little money. It would be cruel kindness to deny it to them; and, in point of fact, except by interfering with the liberty of the subject, it would be impossible to prevent them. Farm-labour is certainly to be preferred to much of the work that women do in manufacturing districts. At least there is no overcrowding; there is plenty of fresh air, and the woman who works in the field looks quite as robust and healthy as her sister sitting all day in a confined factory.

It used to be common to see women dressed in a kind of smock-frock; this was in the days when they milked, and it is still occasionally worn. Now they generally wear linsey dresses in the winter, and cotton in the summer, at prices from 4½d. to 6d. per yard. They wear boots nailed and tipped much like the men, but not so heavy, and in rough weather corduroy gaiters. Their cooking is rude and detestable to any one else's ideas; but it appears exactly suited to the coarse tastes and hearty appetite of their husbands. Being uneducated, and a large proportion unable to read, their chief intellectual amusement consists in tittle-tattle and gossip. They are generally inclined to be religious after a fashion, and frequent the chapel or the cottage in which the itinerant preacher holds forth. In summer this preacher will mount upon a waggon placed in a field by the road-side, and draw a large audience, chiefly women, who loudly respond and groan and mutter after the most approved manner. Now and then an elderly woman may be found who is considered to have a gift of preaching, and holds forth at great length, quoting Scripture right and left. The exhibitions of emotion on the part of the women at such meetings and in the services in their cottages are not pleasant to listen to, but the impression left on the mind is that they are in earnest.

They are a charitable race, and eager to help each other. They will watch by the bedsides of their sick neighbours, divide the loaf of bread, look after the children, and trudge weary miles to the town for medicine. On the other hand, they are almost childlike in imbibing jealousies and hatreds, and unsparing in abuse and imputation towards a supposed enemy. They are bolder in speech than their husbands to those who occupy higher places in the social scale. It cannot be said that agricultural women are handsome. In childhood they are too often thin and stunted; later they shoot up and grow taller, but remain thin and bony till from eighteen to twenty, when they get plumper, and then is their period of prettiness, if at all. Bright eyes, clear complexions, and glossy hair form their attractions, for their features are scarcely ever good. The brief beauty of the prime of youth speedily fades, and at five-and-twenty the agricultural woman, especially if married, is pale or else burnt by the sun to a brown, with flat chest and rounded shoulders. It is rare indeed to see a woman with any pretensions to what is called a figure. It would be wonderful if there were, for much of the labour induces a stooping position, and they are never taught when young to sit upright.

Growing plainer and plainer as years go by, the elder women are wrinkled and worn-looking, and have contracted a perpetual stoop. Many live to a great age. In small parishes it is common to find a large number of women of seventy and eighty, and there are few cottages which do not contain an old woman. This is hardly a result in accordance with the labour they have undergone. The explanation probably is that, continued through a series of generations, it has produced a strength and stamina which can survive almost anything. Certain it is that young couples about to marry often experience much difficulty in finding cottages, because they are occupied by extremely aged pairs; and landlords, anxious to tear down and remove old cottages tumbling to pieces, are restrained from doing so out of regard for the aged tenants, who cling with a species of superstitious tenderness to the crumbling walls and decayed thatch. At this age, at seventy-five or even eighty, the agricultural woman retains a strength of body astonishing to a town-bred woman. She will walk eight or ten miles, without apparent fatigue, to and from the nearest town for her provisions. She will almost to the last carry her prong out into the hayfield, and do a little work in some corner, and bear her part in the gleaning after the harvest. She lives almost entirely upon weak tea and bread sops. Her mental powers continue nearly unimpaired, and her eyes are still good, though her teeth have long gone. She will laugh over memories of practical jokes played at harvest-homes half-a-century ago; and slowly spells over the service in a prayer-book which asks blessings upon a king instead of a queen. She often keeps the village 'confectioner's' shop—*i.e.,* a few bottles of sweets and jumbles in the window, side by side with 'twists' of whipcord for the ploughboys and carters, and perhaps has a license for tobacco and snuff.

But long before this age they have in most cases been kept by the parish. The farmers who form the guardians know well the history of the poor of their parishes, and remembering the long years of hard work, always allow as liberal a relief as they can to these women. Out of all their many children and grandchildren, it may happen that one has got on fairly well in life, has a business as a blacksmith, or tinker, or carpenter, and gives her a shilling or so a week; and a shilling goes a long way with a woman who lives upon tea and sops. In their latter days these women resemble the pollard oaks, which linger on year after year, and finally fall from sheer decay.

AN ENGLISH HOMESTEAD

It is easy to pass along a country road without observing half of the farmhouses, so many being situated at a distance from the highway, and others hidden by the thick hedges and the foliage of the trees. This is especially the case in districts chiefly occupied in pasture farming, meadow land being usually found along the banks of rivers, on broad level plains, or in slightly undulating prairie-like country. A splendid belt of meadows often runs at the base of the chalk hills, where the springs break out; and it is here that some of the most beautiful pastoral scenery is to be found.

By the side of the highway there are gates at intervals in the close-cropped hedge—kept close-cropped by the strict orders of the road surveyors—giving access to the green fields through which runs a waggon-track, apparently losing itself in the grass. This track will take the explorer to a farmhouse. It is not altogether pleasant to drive over in a spring trap, as the wheels jolt in the hard ruts, and the springs are shaken in the deep furrows, the vehicle going up and down like a boat upon the waves. Why there should be such furrows in a meadow is a question that naturally arises in the mind. Whether it be mown with the scythe or the mowing-machine, it is of advantage to have the surface of the field as nearly as possible level; and it is therefore most probable that these deep furrows had their origin at a period when a different state of things prevailed, when the farmer strove to grow as much wheat as possible, and devoted every acre that he dared break up to the plough. Many of these fields were ill adapted for the growth of corn, the soil unsuitable and liable to be partially flooded; consequently as soon as the market was opened, and the price of wheat declined, so that rapid fortunes could no longer be made by it, the fields were allowed to return to their natural condition. No trouble was taken to relevel the land, and the furrows remain silent witnesses to the past. They are useful as drains it is true; but, being so broad, the water only passes off slowly and encourages the rough grass and 'bull-polls' to spring up, which are as uneatable by cattle as the Australian spinifex.

The waggon-track is not altogether creditable to the farmer, who would, one would have thought, have had a good road up to his house at all events. It is very wide, and in damp weather every one who drives along it goes further and further out into the grass to find a firm spot, till as much space is rendered barren as by one of the great hedges, now so abominated. The expense of laying down stone is considerable in some localities where the geological formation does not afford quarries; yet even then there is a plan, simple in itself, but rarely resorted to, by which a great saving in outlay may be effected. Any one who will look at a cart-track will see that there are three parallel marks left by the passage of the cart upon the ground. The two outside ruts are caused by the wheels, and between these is a third beaten in by the hoofs of the horse. The plan consists in placing stone, broken up small, not across the whole width of the track, but in these three ruts only; for it is in these ruts alone that the wear takes place, and, if the ground were firm there, no necessity would exist to go farther into the field. To be thoroughly successful, a trench, say six or eight inches wide, and about as deep, should be cut in the place of each rut, and these trenches macadamised. Grass grows freely in the narrow green strips between the ruts, and the track has something of the appearance of a railroad. It is astonishing how long these metals, as it were, will last, when once well put down; and the track has a neat, effective look. The foot-passenger is as much benefited as the tenant of the field. In wet weather he walks upon the macadamised strip dryshod, and in summer upon either of the grass strips, easily and comfortably, without going out into the mowing-grass to have the pleasure of turf under his feet.

These deep furrows are also awkward to cross with heavy loads of hay or straw, and it requires much skill to build a load able to withstand the severe jolting and lurching. Some of the worst are often filled up with a couple of large faggots in the harvest season. These tracks run by the side of the hedge, and the ditches are crossed by bridges or 'drocks.' The last gate opens into a small field surrounded with a high thick hawthorn hedge, itself a thing of beauty in May and June, first with the May blossom and afterwards with the delicate-tinted dog or wild roses. A spreading ash-tree stands on either side of the gateway, from which on King Charles's day the ploughboys carefully select small branches, those with the leaves evenly arranged, instead of odd numbers, to place in their hats. Tall elm-trees grow close together in the hedge and upon the 'shore' of the ditch, enclosing the place in a high wall of foliage. In the branches are the rooks' nests, built of small twigs apparently thrown together, and yet so firmly intertwined as to stand the swaying of the tree-tops in the rough blasts of winter. In the spring the rook builds a second nest on the floor of the old one, and this continues till five or six successive layers may be traced; and when at last some ruder tempest strews the grass with its ruin, there is enough wood to fill a bushel basket.

The dovecot is fixed in the fork of one of the larger elms, where the trunk divides into huge boughs, each the size of a tree; and in the long rank grass near the hedge the backs of a black Berkshire pig or two may be seen like porpoises rolling in the green sea. Here and there an ancient apple-tree, bent down and bowed to the ground with age, offers a mossy, shady seat upon one of its branches which has returned to the earth from which it sprung. Some wooden posts grown green and lichen-covered, standing at regular intervals, show where the housewife dries her linen. Right before the very door a great horse-chestnut tree rears itself in all the beauty of its thousands of blossoms, hiding half the house. A small patch of ground in front is railed in with wooden palings to keep out the pigs, and poultry, and dogs—for almost every visitor brings with him one or more dogs—and in this narrow garden grow velvety wall-flowers, cloves, pinks, shrubs of lavender, and a few herbs which are useful for seasoning. The house is built of brick; but the colour is toned down by age, and against the wall a pear-tree is trained upon one side, and upon the other a cherry-tree, so that at certain seasons one may rise in the morning and gather the fresh fruits from the window. The lower windows were once latticed; but the old frames have been replaced with the sash, which, if not so picturesque, affords more light, and most old farmhouses are deficient in the supply of light. The upper windows remain latticed still. The red tiles of the roof are dull with lichen and the beating of the weather; and the chimney, if looked at closely, is full of tiny holes—it is where the leaden pellets from guns fired at the mischievous starlings have struck the bricks. A pair of doves perched upon the roof-tree coo amorously to each other, and a thin streak of blue smoke rises into the still air.

The door is ajar, or wide open. There is no fear here of thieves, or street-boys throwing stones into the hall. Excepting in rain or rough wind, and at night, that front door will be open almost all the summer long. When shut at night it is fastened with a wooden bar passing across the whole width of the door, and fitting into iron staples on each post—a simple contrivance, but very strong and not easily tampered with. Many of the interior doors still open with the old thumb-latch; but the piece of shoe-string to pull and lift it is now relegated to the cottages, and fast disappearing even there before brass-handled locks. This house is not old enough to possess the nail-studded door of solid oak and broad stone-built porch of some farmhouses still occasionally to be found, and which date from the sixteenth century. The porch here simply projects about two feet, and is supported by trellis-work, up which the honeysuckle has been trained. A path of stone slabs leads from the palings up to the threshold, and the hall within is paved with similar flags. The staircase is opposite the doorway, narrow, and guiltless of oilcloth or carpeting; and with reason, for the tips and nails of the heavy boots which tramp up and down it would speedily wear carpets into rags. There is a door at the bottom of the staircase closed at night. By the side of the staircase is a doorway which leads into the dairy—two steps lower than the front of the house.

The sitting-room is on the left of the hall, and the floor is of the same cold stone flags, which in damp weather become wet and slimy. These flags, in fact, act as a barometer, and foretell rain with great accuracy, as it were perspiring with latent moisture at its approach. The chimney was originally constructed for a wood fire upon the hearth, and of enormous size, so that several sides of bacon could be hung up inside to be smoke-dried. The fireplace was very broad, so that huge logs could be thrown at once upon the fire with very little trouble of sawing them short. Since coal has come into general use, and wood grown scarce, the fireplace has been partly built up and an iron grate inserted, which looks out of place in so large a cavity. The curious fire-dogs, upon which the wood was thrown, may still, perhaps be found upstairs in some corner of the lumber-room. On the mantelpiece are still preserved, well polished and bright, the several pieces of the 'jack' or cooking apparatus; and a pair of great brazen candlesticks ornament it at each end. A leaden or latten tobacco-bowl, a brazen pestle and mortar, and half-a-dozen odd figures in china, are also scattered upon it, surmounted by a narrow looking-glass. In one corner stands an old eight-day clock with a single hour hand—minute hands being a modern improvement; but it is silent, and its duties are performed by an American time-piece supported upon a bracket against the wall. Upstairs, however, upon the landing, a similar ancient piece of clockmaking still ticks solemn and slow with a ponderous melancholy. The centre of the room is occupied with an oaken table, solid and enduring, but inconvenient to sit at; and upon each side of the fireplace is a stiff-backed arm-chair. A ledge under the window forms a pleasant seat in summer. Before the fireplace is a rug, the favourite resort of the spaniels and cats. The rest of the floor used to be bare; but of late years a square of coconut matting has been laid down. A cumbrous piece of furniture takes up

almost half of one side—not known in modern manu-
factories. It is of oak, rudely polished, and inlaid with
brass. At the bottom are great deep drawers, pulled open
with brass rings ornamented with dogs' heads. In these
drawers are kept cowdrenches—bottles of oils for the
wounds which cattle sometimes get from nails or kicks;
dog-whips and pruning-knives; a shot-belt and powder-
flask; an old horse-pistol; a dozen odd stones or fossils
picked up upon the farm and kept as curiosities; twenty or
thirty old almanacs, and a file of the county paper for forty
years; and a hundred similar odds and ends. Above the
drawers comes a desk with a few pigeon-holes; a desk little
used, for the farmer is less of a literary turn than almost any
other class. The pigeon-holes are stuffed full of old papers,
recipes for cattle medicines, and, perhaps, a book of
divinity or sermons printed in the days of Charles II,
leather-covered and worm-eaten. Still higher are a pair of
cupboards where china, the tea-set, and the sugar and
groceries in immediate use are kept. On the top, which is
three or four inches under the ceiling, are two or three
small brown-paper parcels of grass seeds, and a variety of
nondescript articles. Opposite, on the other wall, and
close above the chimneypiece, so as to be kept dry, is the
gunrack with two double-barrels, a long single-barrel
duck gun, and a cavalry sabre, worn once a year by a son of
the house who goes out to training in the yeomanry.

There are a few pictures, not of a high class—three or
four prints depicting Dick Turpin's ride to York, and a
coloured sketch of some steeplechase winner, or a copy of
a well-known engraving representing a feat accomplished
many years ago at a farm. A flock of sheep were shorn, the
wool carded and spun, and a coat made of it, and worn by
the flockowner, and all in one day. From this room a door

opens into the cellar and pantry, partly underground, and reached by three or four steps.

On the other side of the hall is the parlour, which was originally floored, like the sitting-room, with stone flags, since taken up and replaced by boards. This is carpeted, and contains a comfortable old-fashioned sofa, horse-hair chairs, and upon the side tables may, perhaps, be found a few specimens of valuable old china, made to do duty as flower-vases, and filled with roses. The room has a fresh, sweet smell from the open window and the flowers. It tempts almost irresistibly to repose in the noontide heat of a summer's day.

Upstairs there are two fair-sized bedrooms, furnished with four-post wooden bedsteads. The second flight of stairs, going up to the attic, has also a door at the foot. This house is built upon a simple but effective design, well calculated for the purposes to be served. It resembles two houses placed not end to end, as in a block, but side by side, and each part has a separate roof. Under the front roof, which is somewhat higher than the other, are the living-rooms of the family: sitting-room, parlour, bed-room, and attics, or servants' bedrooms. Under the lower roof are the offices, the cheese-loft, dairy, kitchen, cellar, and wood-house. Numerous doors give easy com-munication on each floor, so that the house consists of two distinct portions, and the business is kept quite apart from the living-rooms, and yet close to them. This is, perhaps, the most convenient manner in which a dairy farmhouse can be built; and the plan was undoubtedly the result of experience. Of course, in dairy-farming upon a very ex-tended scale, or as a gentlemanly amusement, it would be preferable to have the offices entirely apart, and at some distance from the dwelling-house. These remarks apply to an ordinary farm of moderate size.

Leaving the hall by the door at the side of the staircase, two steps descend into the dairy, which is almost invariably floored with stone flags, even in localities where brick is used for the flooring of the sitting-room. The great object aimed at in the construction of the dairy was coolness, and freedom from dust as much as possible. The stone flags ensure a cool floor; and the windows always open to the north, so that neither the summer sunshine nor the warm southern winds can injuriously affect the produce. It is a long open room, whitewashed, in the centre of which stands the cheese-tub, until lately invariably made of wood, but now frequently of tin, this material taking much less trouble to keep clean. The cheese-tub is large enough for a Roman lady's bath of milk. Against one wall are the whey-leads—shallow, long, and broad vessels of wood, lined with lead, supported two or three feet above the floor, so that buckets can be placed underneath. In these 'leads' the whey is kept, and drawn off by pulling up a wooden plug. Under the 'leads'—as out of the way—are some of the great milk-pans into which the milk is poured. Pussy sometimes dips her nose into these, and whitens her whiskers with cream. At one end of the room is the cheese-press. The ancient press, with its complicated arrangement of long iron levers weighted at the end something like a steelyard, and drawn up by cords and pulleys, has been taken down and lies discarded in the lumber-room. The pressure in the more modern machine is obtained from a screw. The rennet-vat is perhaps hidden behind the press, and there are piles of the cheese-moulds or vats beside it, into which the curd is placed when fit to be compressed into the proper shape and consistency. All the utensils here are polished, and clean to the last degree;

without extreme cleanliness success in cheese or butter making cannot be achieved. The windows are devoid of glass; they are really wind doors, closed when necessary, with a shutter on hinges like a cupboard door. Cats and birds are prevented from entering by means of wire screens—like a coarse netting of wire—and an upright iron bar keeps out more dangerous thieves. There is a copper for scalding milk. When in good order there is scarcely any odour in a dairy, notwithstanding the decidedly strong smell of some of the materials employed: free egress of air and perfect cleanliness takes off all but the faintest *astringent* flavour. In summer it is often the custom of dairymaids to leave buckets full of water standing under the 'leads' or elsewhere out of the way, or a milk-pan is left with water in it, to purify the atmosphere. Water, it is well known, has a remarkable power of preventing the air from going 'dead' as it were. A model dairy should have a small fountain in some convenient position, with a jet constantly playing. The state of the atmosphere has the most power-ful effect upon the contents of the dairy, especially during times of electrical tension.

To the right of the dairy is the brewhouse, now rarely used for the purpose implied in its name, though the tubs, and coolers, and other 'plant' necessary for the process are still preserved. Here there is a large copper also; and the oven often opens on to the brewhouse. In this place the men have their meals. Next to it is the wood-house, used for the storage of the wood which is required for im-mediate use, and must therefore be dry; and beyond that the kitchen, where the fire is still upon the hearth, though coal is mixed with the logs and faggots. Along the whole length of this side of the house there is a paved or pitched courtyard enclosed by a low brick wall, with one or two gates opening upon the paths which lead to the rickyards and the stalls. The buttermilk and refuse from the dairy runs by a channel cut in the stone across the court into a vault or well sunk in the ground, from whence it is dipped for the pigs. The vault is closed at the mouth by a heavy wooden lid. There is a well and pump for water here; sometimes with a windlass, when the well is deep. If the water be low or out of condition, it is fetched in yokes from the nearest running stream. The acid or 'eating' power of the buttermilk, &c., may be noted in the stones, which in many places are scooped or hollowed out. A portion of the court is roofed in, and is called the 'skilling.' It is merely covered in without walls, the roof supported upon oaken posts. Under this the buckets are placed to dry after being cleaned, and here the churn may often be seen. A separate staircase, rising from the dairy, gives access to the cheese-loft. It is an immense apartment, reaching from one end of the house to the other, and as lofty as the roof will permit, for it is not ceiled. The windows are like those of the dairy. Down the centre are long double shelves sustained upon strong upright beams, tier upon tier from the floor as high as the arms can conveniently reach. Upon these shelves the cheese is stored, each lying upon its side; and, as no two cheeses are placed one upon the other until quite ready for eating, a ton or two occupies a considerable space while in process of drying. They are also placed in rows upon the floor, which is made exceptionally strong, and supported upon great beams to bear the weight. The scales used to be hung from a beam overhead, and consisted of an iron bar, at each end of which a square board was slung with ropes— one board to pile up the cheese on, and the other for the counterpoise of weights. These rude and primitive scales are now generally superseded by modern and more accurate instruments, weighing to a much smaller fraction. Stone half-hundred-weights and stone quarters were in common use not long since. A cheese-loft, when full, is a noble sight of its kind, and represents no little labour and skill. When sold, the cheese is carefully packed in the cart with straw to prevent its being injured. The oil or grease from the cheese gradually works its way into the shelves and floor, and even into the staircase, till the woodwork seems saturated with it. Rats and mice are the pests of the loft; and so great is their passion for cheese that neither cats, traps, nor poison can wholly repress these invaders, against whom unceasing war is waged. The starlings—who, if the roof be of thatch, as it is in many farmhouses, make their nests in it—occasionally carry their holes right through, and are unmercifully exterminated when they venture within reach, or they would quickly let the rain and the daylight in.

As the dairy and offices face the north, so the front of the house—the portion used for domestic purposes—has a southern aspect, which experience has proved to be healthy. But at the same time, despite its compactness and general convenience, there are many defects in the building—defects chiefly of a sanitary character. It is very doubtful if there are any drains at all. Even though the soil be naturally dry, the ground floor is almost always cold and damp. The stone flags are themselves cold enough, and are often placed upon the bare earth. The threshold is on a level with the ground outside, and sometimes a step lower, and in wet weather the water penetrates to the hall. There is another disadvantage. If the door be left open, which it usually is, frogs, toads, and creeping things generally, sometimes make their way in, though ruthlessly swept out again; and an occasional snake from the long grass at the very door is an unpleasant, though perfectly harmless visitor. The floor should be raised a foot or so above the level of the earth, and some provision made against the damp by a layer of concrete or something of the kind. If not, even if boards be substituted for the flags, they will soon decay. It often happens that farmhouses upon meadow land are situated on low ground, which in winter is saturated with water which stands in the furrows, and makes the footpaths leading to the house impassable except to water-tight boots. This must, and undoubtedly does affect the health of the inmates, and hence probably the prevalence of rheumatism. The site upon which the house stands should be so drained as to carry off the water. Some soils contract to an appreciable extent in a continuance of drought, and expand in an equal degree with wet—a fact apparent to any one who walks across a field where the soil is clay, in a dry time, when the deep, wide cracks cannot be overlooked. Alternate swelling and contraction of the earth under the foundations of a house produce a partial dislocation of the brickwork, and hence it is common enough to see cracks running up the walls. Had the site been properly drained, and the earth consequently always dry, this would not have happened; and it is a matter of consideration for the landlord, who in time may find it necessary to shore up a wall with a buttress. The great difference in the temperature of a drained soil and an undrained one has often been observed, amounting sometimes to as much as twenty degrees—a serious matter where health is concerned. A foolish custom was observed in the building of many old farmhouses, *i.e.*, of carrying beams of wood across the chimney—a practice that has led to disastrous fires. The soot accumulates. These huge

cavernous chimneys are rarely swept, and at last catch
alight and smoulder for many days; presently fire breaks
out in the middle of a room under which the beam passes.

Houses erected in blocks or in towns do not encounter
the full force of the storms of winter to the same degree as a
solitary farmhouse, standing a quarter or half-a-mile from
any other dwelling. This is the reason why the old farmers
planted elm-trees and encouraged the growth of thick
hawthorn hedges close to the homestead. The north-east
and the south-west are the quarters from whence most is
to be dreaded: the north-east for the bitter wind which
sweeps along and grows colder from the damp, wet
meadows it passes over; and the south-west for the driving
rain, lasting sometimes for days and weeks together. Trees
and hedges break the force of the gales, and in summer
shelter from the glaring sun.

The architectural arrangement of the farmhouse just
described gives almost perfect privacy. Except visitors, no
one comes to the front door or passes unpleasantly close to
the windows. Labourers and others all go to the courtyard
at the back. The other plans upon which farmsteads are
built are far from affording similar privacy. There are
some which, in fact, are nothing but an enlarged and
somewhat elongated cottage, with the dwelling-rooms at
one end and the dairy and offices at the other, and the
bedrooms over both. Everybody and everything brought
to or taken from the place has to pass before the dwel-
ling-room windows—a most unpleasant arrangement.
Another style is square, with low stone walls white-
washed, and thatched roof of immense height. Against it is
a lean-to, the eaves of the roof of which are hardly three
feet from the ground. So high-pitched a roof necessitates
the employment of a great amount of woodwork, and the

upper rooms have sloping ceilings. They may look picturesque from a distance, but are inconvenient and uncouth within, and admirably calculated for burning. A somewhat superior description is built in the shape of a carpenter's 'square.' The dwelling-rooms form, as it were, one house, and the offices, dairy and cheese-loft are added on at right angles. The courtyard is in the triangular space between. For some things this is a convenient arrangement; but there still remains the disagreeableness of the noise, and, at times, strong odours from the courtyard under the windows of the dwelling-house. Nearly all farmsteads have awkwardly low ceilings, which in a town would cause a close atmosphere, but are not so injurious in the open country, with doors constantly ajar. In erecting a modern house this defect would, of course, be avoided. The great thickness of the walls is sometimes a deception; for in pulling down old buildings it is occasionally found that the interior of the wall is nothing but loose broken stones and bricks enclosed or rammed in between two walls. The staircases are generally one of the worst features of the old houses, being between a wall and a partition—narrow, dark, steep, and awkwardly placed, and without windows or handrails. These houses were obviously built for a people living much out of doors.

JOHN SMITH'S SHANTY

HE was standing in the ditch leaning heavily upon the long handle of his axe. It was a straight stick of ash, roughly shaved down to some sort of semblance of smoothness, such as would have worked up an unpractised hand into a mass of blisters in ten minutes' usage, but which glided easily through those horny palms, leaving no mark of friction. The continuous outdoor labour, the beating of innumerable storms, and the hard, coarse fare, had dried up all the original moisture of the hand, till it was rough, firm, and cracked or chapped like a piece of wood exposed to the sun and weather. The natural oil of the skin, which gives to the hand its beautiful suppleness and delicate sense of touch, was gone like the sap in the tree he was felling, for it was early in the winter. However the brow might perspire, there was no dampness on the hand and the helve of the axe was scarcely harder and drier. In order, therefore, that the grasp might be firm, it was necessary to artificially wet the palms, and hence the custom which so often disgusts lookers-on, of spitting on the hands before commencing work. This apparently gratuitous piece of dirtiness is in reality absolutely necessary. Men with hands in this state have hardly any feeling in them; they find it difficult to pick up anything small, as a pin—the fingers fumble over it; as for a pen, they hold it like a hammer. His chest was open to the north wind, which whistled through the bare branches of the tall elm overhead as if they were the cordage of a ship, and came in sudden blasts through the gaps in the hedge, blowing his shirt back, and exposing the immense breadth of bone, and rough dark skin tanned to a brown-red by the summer sun while mowing. The neck rose from it short and thick like that of a bull, and the head was round, and covered with a crop of short grizzled hair not yet quite grey, but fast losing its original chestnut colour. The features were fairly regular, but coarse, and the nose flattened. An almost worn-out old hat thrown back on the head showed a low, broad, wrinkled forehead. The eyes were small and bleared, set deep under shaggy eyebrows. The corduroy trousers, yellow with clay and sand, were shortened below the knee by leather straps like garters, so as to exhibit the whole of the clumsy boots, with soles like planks, and shod with iron at heel and tip. These boots weigh seven pounds the pair; and in wet weather, with clay and dirt clinging to them, must reach nearly double that.

In spite of all the magnificent muscular development which this man possessed, there was nothing of the Hercules about him. The grace of strength was wanting, the curved lines were lacking; all was gaunt, angular, and square. The chest was broad enough, but flat, a framework of bones hidden by a rough hairy skin; the breasts did not swell up like the rounded prominences of the antique statue. The neck strong enough as it was to bear the weight of a sack of corn with ease, was too short, and too much a part, as it were, of the shoulders. It did not rise up like a tower, distinct in itself; and the muscles on it, as they moved, produced hollow cavities distressing to the eye. It was strength without beauty; a mechanical kind of power, like that of an engine, working through straight lines and sharp angles. There was too much of the machine, and too little of the animal; the lithe, easy motion of the lion or the tiger was not there. The impression conveyed was, that such strength had been gained through a course of incessant exertion of the rudest kind, unassisted by generous food and checked by unnatural exposure.

John Smith heaved up his axe and struck at the great bulging roots of the elm, from which he had cleared away the earth with his spade. A heavy chip flew out with a dull thud on the sward. The straight handle of the axe increased the labour of the work, for in this curiously conservative country the American improvement of the double curved handle has not yet been adopted. Chip after chip fell in the ditch, or went spinning out into the field. The axe rose and fell with slow, monotonous motion. Though there was immense strength in every blow, there was no vigour in it. Suddenly, while it was swinging in the air overhead, there came the faint, low echo of a distant railway whistle, and the axe was dropped at once, without even completing the blow. 'That's the express,' he muttered, and began cleaning the dirt from his shoes. The daily whistle of the express was the signal for luncheon. Hastily throwing on a slop hung on the bushes, and over that a coat, he picked up a small bag, and walked slowly off down the side of the hedge to where the highway road went by. Here he sat down, somewhat sheltered by a hawthorn bush, in the ditch, facing the road, and drew out his bread and cheese.

About a quarter of a loaf of bread, or nearly, and one slice of cheese was this full-grown and powerful man's dinner that cold, raw winter's day. His drink was a pint of cold weak tea, kept in a tin can, for these men are moderate enough with liquor at their meals, whatever they may be at other times. He held the bread with his left hand and the cheese was placed on it, and kept in its place by thumb, the grimy dirt on which was shielded by a small piece of bread beneath it from the precious cheese. His plate and dish was his broad palm, his only implement a great jack-knife with a buck-horn handle. He ate slowly, thoughtfully, deliberately; weighing each mouthful, chewing the cud as it were. All the man's motions were heavy and slow, deadened as if clogged with a great load. There was no 'life' in him. What little animation there was left had taken him to eat his dinner by the roadside—the instinct of sociality—that if possible he might exchange a word with some one passing. In factories men work in gangs, and hundreds are often within call of each other; a rough joke or an occasional question can be put and answered; there is a certain amount of sympathy, a sensation of company and companionship. But alone in the fields, the human instinct of friendship is checked, the man is driven back upon himself and his own narrow range of thought, till the mind and heart grow dull, and there only remains such a vague ill-defined want as carried John Smith to the roadside that day.

He had finished his cheese and lit a short clay pipe, and thrust his hands deep in his pockets, when there was a rustling noise in the hedge a little farther down, and a short man jumped out into the road—even jumping with his hands in his pockets. He saw Smith directly and came towards him, and sat himself on a heap of flints used for mending the road.

'What's thee at to-day?' asked John, after a pause.

'Ditching,' said the other laconically, pushing out one foot by way of illustrating the fact. It was covered with black mud far above the ankle, and there were splashes of mud up to his waist—his hands, as he proceeded to light his pipe, were black too, from the same cause.

'Thee's bin in main deep,' said John, after a slow survey of the other's appearance.

The fellow stamped his boot on the ground, and the slime and slush oozed out of it and formed a puddle. 'That's pretty stuff to stand in for a man of sixty-four, yent it, John?' With a volubility and energy of speech little to be expected from his wizened appearance, the hedger and ditcher entered into details of his job. He began work at six that morning with stiff legs and swollen feet, and as he stood in the mingled mire and water, the rheumatism came gradually on, rising higher up his limbs from the ankles, and growing sharper with every twinge, while the cold and bitter wind cut through his thin slop on his chest, which was not so strong as it used to be. His arms got stiff with the labour of lifting up shovelful after shovelful of heavy mud to plaster the side of the ditch, his feet turned cold as 'flints,' and the sickly smell of the slime upset his stomach so that when he tried to eat his bread and cheese he could not. Through this speech John smoked steadily on, till the other stopped and looked at him for sympathy.

'Well, Jim, anyhow,' said Smith, 'thee hasn't got far to walk to the job;' and he pointed with the stem of his pipe to the low roof of a cottage just visible a few hundred yards distant.

'Ay, and a place it be to live in, that,' said Jim. There were only two rooms, he explained, and both downstairs —no upstairs at all—and the first of these was so small he could reach across it, and the thatch had got so thin in one place that the rain came through. The floor was only hard mud, and the garden not big enough to grow a sack of potatoes, while one wall of the house, which was only 'wattle and daub' (*i.e.*, lath and plaster), rose up from the very edge of a great stagnant pond. Overhead there was an elm, from the branches of which in wet weather there was a perpetual drip, drip, on the thatch, till the moss and grass grew on the roof in profusion. All the sewage and drainage from the cottage ran into the pond, over which at night there was almost always a thick damp mist, which crept in through the crevices of the rotten walls, and froze the blood in the sleepers' veins. Sometimes a flood came down, and the pond rose and washed away the cabbages from the garden, leaving a deposit of gritty sand which killed all vegetation, and they could only keep the water from coming indoors by making a small dam of clay across the doorway. There was only a low hedge of elder between the cottage and a dirty lane; and in the night, especially if there happened to be a light burning, it was common enough for a stone to come through the window, flung by some half-drunken ploughboy. A pretty place for a human being to live in: and again he looked up into Smith's face for comment.

'Thee built 'un thee-self, didn't 'ee?' said John, in his slow way.

'Ay, that I did,' continued Jim, not seeing the drift of the remark. He not only built it, but he brought up nineteen children in it, and fourteen of them lived to grow up, all the offspring of one wife. And a time she had of it, too. None of them ever fell in that pond, though he often wished they would; and they were all pretty healthy, which was a bad thing, because it made them hungry, and if they had been ill the parish would have kept them. All that he had done on 12s. a week, and he minded the time when it was only 9s., ay, and even when it was 6s., and 'twas better then than it was now with 15s. That was before the Unions came about, in the time of the old workhouses in every parish. Then the farmers used to find everybody a job. Every morning they had to go round from one farmer to the other, and if there was no work then they went to the workhouse, or sometimes to the vestry-room in the church, where every man had a loaf of bread for every head there was in his family, so that the more children he had the more loaves of bread, which was a capital thing when the children were small. He had known a man in those times sent seven miles with a wheelbarrow to fetch a barrow load of coal from the canal wharf, and then have to wheel it back seven miles, and get one shilling for his day's work. Still they were better times than these, because the farmers for their own sake were forced to find the fellows something to do; but now they did not care, and it was a hard thing to find work, especially when a man grew old, and stiff about the joints. Now the Boards of Guardians would not give any relief unless the applicants were ill, or not able-bodied, and even then they were often required to break stones, and he was very much inclined to throw his spade in that old pond and go to the Union with the 'missis' and all the lot for good. He had the rheumatism bad enough. It would serve them right. He had worked 'nigh handy' sixty years; and all he had got by it he could put in his eye. They ought to keep him now. It was not half so good as the old times for all the talk; then the children could bring home a bit of wood out of the hedges to boil the pot with, but now they must not touch a stick, or there was the law on them in a minute. And then coal at the price it was. Why didn't his sons keep him? Where were they? One was a soldier, and another had gone to America, and the third was married and had a hard job to keep himself, and the fourth was gone nobody knew where. As for the wenches, they were no good in that way. So he and his 'missis' muddled on at home with three of the youngest. And they could not let them alone even in that. He did go into the Union workhouse for a bit, a while ago, when the rheumatism was extraordinary bad, but some of the guardians smelt out that he had a cottage of his own, and it was against the law to relieve anybody that had property; so he must pay back the relief as a loan or sell the cottage. He was offered £25 for the place and garden, and he meant to have taken it, but when they came to look into the writings it was not clear that he could sell it. It was a quit-rent land, and although the landlord had not taken the rent for twenty years, yet he had entered it in his book as paid (out of good nature), and the lawyers said it could not be done. But as they would not let him sell it, he would not turn out, not he. There he would stop—just to spite them. He knew that nook of his was wanted for cattle stalls on the new principle, and very handy it would be with all that water close at hand, but he had worked for sixty years, and had had nineteen children there, and he would not turn out. Not he. The parson's 'missis' and the squire's 'missis' came the other day about the youngest boy of his. They wanted to get him into some school up in London somewhere, but he remembered how the squire had served him just for picking up a dead rabbit that laid in his path one hard snow time. Six weeks in gaol because he could not pay the fine. And the parson turned him out of his allotment because he saw him stagger a little in the road one night with rheumatism. It was a lie that he was drunk. And suppose he was? The parson had his wine, he reckoned. They should not have his boy. He rather hoped he would grow up a bad one, and bother them well. He minded when that sharp old Miss — was always coming round with tracts and blankets, like taking some straw to a lot of pigs, and lecturing his 'missis' about economy. What a fuss she made, and scolded his wife as if she was a thief for having that fifteenth boy! His 'missis' turned on her at last, and said, 'Lor, miss, that's all the pleasure me an' my old man got.' As for this talk about the labourers' Unions, it was all very well for the young men; but it made it worse still for the old ones. The farmers, if they had to give such a price, would have young men in full strength; there was no chance at all for an old fellow of sixty-four with rheumatism. Some of them, too, were terribly offended—some of the old sort—and turned off the few pensioners they had kept on at odd jobs for years. However, he supposed he must get back to that ditch again.

This long oration was delivered not without a certain degree of power and effect, showing that the man, whatever his faults, might with training have become rather a clever fellow. The very way in which he contradicted himself, and announced his intention of never doing that which a moment before he was determined on, was not without an amount of oratorical art, since the turn in his view of the subject was led up to by a variety of reasons which were supposed to convince himself and his hearer at the same time. His remarks were all the more effective because there was an evident substratum of stern truth beneath them. But they failed to make much impression on Smith, who saw his companion depart without a word.

The fact was, that Smith was too well acquainted with the private life of the orator. In his dull, dim way, he half recognised that the unfortunate old fellow's evils had been in great part of his own creating. He knew that he was far from faultless. That poaching business—a very venial offence in a labourer's eyes—he knew had been a serious one, a matter of some two-score pheasants and a desperate fight with a gang. Looking at it as property, the squire had been merciful, pleading with the magistrates for a mitigated penalty. The drunkenness was habitual. In short, they were a bad lot—there was a name attached to the whole family for thieving, poaching, drinking, and even worse. Yet still there were two points that did sink deep into Smith's mind, and made him pause several times that afternoon in his work. The first was that long family of nineteen mouths, with the father and mother making twenty-one. What a number of sins, in the rude logic of the struggle for existence, that terrible fact glossed over! Who could blame—what labourer at least could blame— the ragged, ill-clothed children for taking the dead wood from the hedges to warm their naked limbs? What labourer could blame the father for taking the hares and rabbits running across his very path to fill that wretched hovel with savoury steam from the pot? And further, what labourer could blame the miserable old man for drowning his feelings, and his sensation of cold and hunger, in liquor?

The great evil of these things is that a fellow-feeling will arise with the wrongdoer, till the original distinction between right and wrong is lost sight of entirely. John Smith had a family too. The other point was the sixty years of labour and their fruit. After two generations of hardest toil and rudest exposure, still dependent upon the seasons even to permit him to work, when that work could be obtained. No rest, no cosy fireside nook: still the bitter wind, and the half-frozen slime and slush rising above the ankle. In an undefined way Smith had been proud of his broad, enormous strength, and rocklike hardihood. He had felt a certain rude pleasure in opening his broad chest to the winter wind. But now he involuntarily closed his shirt and buttoned it. He did not feel so confident in his own power of meeting all the contingencies of the future.

Thought without method and without logical sequence is apt to press heavily upon the uneducated mind. It was thus that these reflections left a sensation of weight and discomfort upon Smith, and it was in a worse humour than was common to his usually well-balanced organisation that he hid away his tools under the bushes as the evening grew too dark for work, and slowly paced homewards. He had some two miles to walk, and he had long since begun to feel hungry. Plodding along in a heavy, uneven gait, there overtook him a tall, raw young lad of eighteen or twenty, slouching forward with vast strides and whistling merrily. The lad slackened his steps and joined company!

'Where bist thee working now, then?' asked Smith.

He replied, evidently in high spirits, that he had that day got a job at the new railway that was making. The wages were 18s. a week—3s. a day—and he had heard that as soon as the men grew to understand their work and to be a little skilful, they could get 24s. easily, up by London. The only drawback was the long walk to the work. Lodgings close at hand were very dear, as also was food, so dear as to lower the actual receipts to an equality, if not below that of the agricultural labourer. Four miles every morning and every night was the price he paid for 18s. a week.

Smith began in his slow, dull way to reckon up his wages aloud against this. First he had 13s. a week for his daily work. Then he had 1s. extra for milking on Sundays, and two good meals with beer on that day. Every weekday he had a pint of beer on finishing work. The young navvy had to find his own liquor. His cottage, it was true, was his own (that is, he only paid a low quit-rent of 1s. a year for it), so that that could not be reckoned in as part of his earnings, as it could with many other men. But the navvy's wages were the same all the year round, while his in summer were often nearly double. As a stalwart mower he could earn 25s. a week and more, as a haymaker 18s., and at harvesting perhaps 30s. If the season was good, and there was a press for hands, he would get more. But, looking forward, there was no prospect of rising higher in his trade, of getting higher wages for more skilful work. He could not be more skilful than he was in ordinary farm work; and as yet the call for clever men to attend to machinery, &c., was very limited; nor were such a class of workmen usually drawn from the resident population where improvements were introduced. The only hope of higher wages that was held out to him was from the gradual rise of everything, or the forced rise consequent upon agitation. But, said he, the navvy must follow his work from place to place, and lodgings are dear in the towns, and the farmers in country places will not let their cottages except to their own labourers—how was the navvy even with higher wages to keep a wife? The aspiring young fellow beside him replied at once sharply and decisively, that he did not mean to have a wife, leastways not till he had got his regular 30s. a week, which he might in time. Then John Smith made a noise in his chest like a grunt.

They parted after this. Smith went into the farmhouse, and got his pint of beer, drinking it in one long slow draught, and then made his way through the scattered village to his cottage. There was a frown on his forehead as he lifted the latch of the long low thatched building which was his home.

The flickering light of the fire on the hearth, throwing great shadows as it blazed up and fell, dazed his eyes as he stepped in, and he did not notice a line stretched right across the room on which small articles of clothing were hanging to dry in a row. A damp worsted stocking flapped against his face, and his foot stumbled on the uneven flag stones which formed the floor. He sat down silently upon a three-legged stool—an old milking-stool—and, putting his hands on his knees, stared into the fire. It was formed of a few sticks with just one knob of coal balanced on the top of them, evident care having been taken that not a jot of its precious heat should be lost. A great black pot with open lid swung over it, from which rose a slight steam and a bubbling noise; this huge, gaunt, bareboned, hungry man, looking into it, saw a large raw swede, just as from the field, with only the greens cut off, simmering for his supper. That root in its day of life had been fed well with superphosphate, and flourished exceedingly, till now its globe could hardly go into the pot. Down the low chimney there came the monotonous growl of the bitter winter wind, and a few spots of rain fell hissing on the embers.

'Is this all thee has got?' he asked, turning to a woman who was busied with some more damp clothes in a basket.

She faced round quickly—a short, narrow, meagre creature, flat-chested and square-shouldered, whose face was the hue of light-coloured clay, an almost corpse-like complexion. Her thin lips hissed out, 'Ay, if thee takes thee money to the pothouse thee won't get bacon for supper.'

Smith said nothing in reply, but stared again into the fire.

The children's voices, which had lowered the moment there seemed a coming quarrel between their parents, rose again. There were three of them—the youngest four, the eldest seven—playing on the stone flags of the floor, between whose rough edges there were wide crevices of hardened mud. With a few short sticks and a broken piece of earthenware for toys, they were happy in their way. Whatever their food might have been, they showed no traces of hard usage. Their red 'puddy' fists were fat, and their naked legs round and plump enough. Their faces were full and rosy, and their voices clear and anything but querulous. The eager passions of childhood came out fierce and unrestrained, and blows were freely interchanged, without however, either cries or apparent hatred. Their naked knees were on the stone-flags, and the wind, creeping in a draught under the ill-fitting door, blew their ragged clothes about.

'Thee med well look at 'em, John,' said the woman, seeing Smith cast a sideway glance at the children; and rapidly manipulating the clothing, her thin nervous lips poured forth a torrent of words upon the silent man. They had had nothing but bread that day, and nothing but bread and lard the day before, and now the lard was gone, and the baker would not trust any more. There were no potatoes because the disease had destroyed them, and the cabbages were sold for that bit of coal; and as for the swede, she took it out of Mr. —'s field, and he was a cross-grained man, and who knew but what they might have the constable on them before morning? Jane W. and Sarah Y. went to prison for seven days for stealing swedes. All along of that cursed drink. If she were the squire she'd shut up all the pothouses in the county. The men went there, and drank the very shirts off their backs, and the clothes off their children, ay, and the shoes off their feet; and what was the use of their having more money when it only went into the publican's pocket? There they sat, and drank the bread out of the babies' mouths. As for the women, the most of them, poor things, never tasted beer from one year's end to another. Old Carter handed her a pint that day, and when she tasted it she did not know what it was. He might smile, but it was true though: no more did Jane W. and Sally Y.: they did not know what it tasted like. And yet they had to be out in the fields at work at eight o'clock, and their washing to do before that, and perhaps a baby in their arms, and the tea as weak as water, and no sugar. Milk, they could not get milk for money— he knew that very well; all the milk went to London. A precious lot of good the higher wages had done them. The farmers would not let them have a drop of milk or a scrap of victuals, and talked about raising the price of the allotment grounds. Allotment, did she say? and how did he lose his allotment?—didn't he drink, drink, drink, till he had to hand over his allotment to the landlord of the pothouse, and did not they take it away from both as soon as they heard of it? Served him right. They had not got a pound of potatoes, and the children did use to lick up the potato-pot liquor as if they liked it.

Smith asked where Polly was, but that was only a signal for a fresh outburst. Polly, if he'd a looked after her she would have been all right. (Smith turned a sharp glance at her in some alarm at this.) Letting a great girl like that go about at night by herself while he was a drink, drink, drinking, and there she was now, a bad hussy, gone to the workhouse to lie in. (Smith winced.) *She* never disgraced herself like that; and if he had sent the wench to service, or stopped her going down to that pothouse with the fellows, this would not have happened. She always told him how it would end. He was a good-for-nothing, drunken brute of a man, and had brought her to all this misery; and she began sobbing.

After twelve long hours of toil, including the walk to and fro, exposed to the bitter cold, with but a slice of cheese to support the strength of that brawny chest, this welcome to his supper was more than the sturdy, silent man could bear. With a dull remembrance of a happy sunlit summer, twenty years ago, when Martha was a plump, laughing girl, of sloe-black eyes and nut-brown complexion—with a glimpse of that merry courting time passing across his mind, Smith got up and walked out into the dark rainy night. 'Ay, thee bist agoing to the liquor again,' were the last words he heard as he shut the door.

It was too true. But what labourer, let us ask, with a full conception of the circumstances, would blame him? Here there was nothing but hard and scanty fare, no heat, no light, nothing to cheer the heart, nothing to cause it to forget the toil of the day and the thought of the morrow, no generous liquor sung by poets to warm the physical man. But only a few yards farther down the road there was a great house, with its shutters cosily closed, ablaze with heat and light, echoing with merry laughter and song. There was an array of good fellows ready to welcome him, to tell him the news, to listen eagerly to what he could tell them, to ask him to drink, and to drink from his cup in boon companionship. There was a social circle in which his heart and intellect could expand, at least for a while, till the strong liquor mounted up and overcame his brain; and then, even then, there was the forgetfulness, the deep slumber of intoxication, utterly oblivious of all things— perhaps the greatest pleasure of all. Smith went there, and who of his own class would blame him? And if his own class did not, of what use is it for other and higher classes to

preach morality to him? It is a man's own comrades, his
own class, whose opinions he dreads and conforms to. If
they condemned him for going there, he would avoid the
public-house. But they would have called him a fool if he
avoided it. In their logic who could say they were wrong?
A man who is happy is a long while getting drunk, he talks
as much as he drinks; but Smith was dull and silent, and
drank steadily. It was not late, but when the house closed
he could but just keep his feet. In the thick darkness and the
driving rain he staggered on, unconscious of the road he
was taking, but bearing roughly towards home. The cold
air rather more stupefied him than brought him to himself.
Insensibly he wandered with uncertain steps down a lane
which led by a gentle slope out into the fields, the fall of the
ground guiding his footsteps, and then stumbling over the
root of an ash-tree, fell heavily on the wet grass. His eyes,
half-shut before, closed as if by clockwork, and in a moment he was firm asleep. His hat had fallen from his brow,
and the grizzled hair was blown about by the wind as it
came in gusts through the hedge. His body was a little
sheltered by the tree, but his chest was open and bare
half-way down his waistcoat; and the heavy drops fell
from the boughs of the ash on his stalwart neck, gradually
saturating his shirt. It may have been that the cold numbed
him and rendered him more insensible than he otherwise
would have been. No star shone out that night; all was
darkness, clouds, and rain till the dawn broke.

Soon after dawn, the young navvy, going to his work
by a short cut, found Smith still asleep, and shook him till
he got up. He was stupid beyond all power of words to
express; but at last came to a dim idea that he must get
home. Then the young navvy left him, anxious about
being late at his employment, and John Smith slowly *felt*

his way to his own door. His wife, already up, opened it. 'Thee varmint! thee never gi'ed I that shilling last night for the baker.' Smith felt hopelessly in his pocket, and then looked at her vacantly. 'Thee drunken, nasty old —,' said the infuriated woman, almost unconsciously lifting her hand. Perhaps it was the action of hers which suggested the same in his mind, which was in a mechanical state. Perhaps the stinging words of last night had at last sunk deep enough to scarify his self-esteem. Perhaps he did not at that moment fully remember the strength of his own mighty arm. But he struck her, and she fell. Her forehead came in contact with the cradle, in which the youngest boy was sleeping, and woke him with a cry. She lay quite still. Smith sat stupidly down on the old milking-stool, with his elbows on his knees. The shrill voice of his wife, as she met him at the door, had brought more than one female neighbour to the window; they saw what happened, and they were there in a minute. Martha was only insensible, and they soon brought her to, but the mark on the temple remained.

Five days afterwards John Smith, agricultural labourer, aged forty-five, stood in the dock to answer a charge of assaulting his wife. There were five magistrates on the Bench—two large landowners, a baronet in the chair, and two clergymen. Martha Smith hung her head as they placed her in the witness-box, and tried to evade kissing the Book, but the police saw that that formality was complied with. The Clerk asked her what she had to complain of. No answer. 'Come, tell us all about it,' said the eldest of the magistrates in a fatherly tone of voice. Still silence. 'Well, how did you get that mark on your forehead?' asked the Clerk. No answer. 'Speak up!' cried a shrill voice in the body of the court. It was one of Martha's cronies, who was immediately silenced by the police; but the train had been fired. Martha would not fail before another woman. But she did not commence about the assault. It was the drink she spoke of, nothing but the drink; and as she talked of that she warmed with her subject and her grievances, and forgot the old love for her husband, and her former hesitation, and placed that vice in all its naked deformity and hideous results in plain but burning words before the Bench. Had she been the cleverest advocate she could not have prepared the ground for her case better. This tale of drink predisposed their minds against the defendant. Only the Clerk, wedded to legal forms, fidgeted under this eloquence, and seized the first pause: 'But now, how about the assault? Come to that,' he said sharply. 'I'm coming, sir,' said Martha; and she described Smith coming home, stupid and ferocious, after staying out all night, and felling her to the ground because she asked him for a shilling to buy the children's daily bread. Then she pointed to the bruise on her forehead, and a suppressed murmur of indignation ran through the Court, and angry looks were directed at the defendant. Did she do or say anything to provoke the blow? asked the Chairman. No more than to ask for the shilling. Did she not abuse him? Well, yes, she did; she owned she did call him a drunken brute afterwards; she could not help it. These women, with their rapid tongues, have a terrible advantage over the slower-witted men.

Had the defendant any questions to ask his wife? Smith began to say that he was very sorry, sir, but the Clerk snapped him up short. 'That's your defence. Have you any questions? No; well, call your witnesses.' Martha called her witnesses, the women living next door. They did not do her case much good; they were too evidently eager to obtain the defendant's condemnation. But, on the other hand, they did not do it any harm, for in the main it was easy to see that they really corroborated her statements. Smith asked them no questions; the labouring class rarely understand the object of cross-questioning. If asked to do so they almost invariably begin to tell their own tale.

'Now, then,' said the Clerk, 'what have you got to say for yourself—what's your defence?' Smith looked down and stammered something. He was confused; they checked him from telling his story when his mouth was full of language, now it would not come. He did not know but that if he began he might be checked again. The eldest magistrate on the Bench saw his embarrassment, and, willing to assist him, spoke as kindly as he could under the circumstances. 'Speak up, John; tell us all about it. I am sorry to see you there.' 'He's the finest, most stalwart man in my parish,' he continued, turning to the Chairman. Thus encouraged, John got out a word or two. He was very sorry; he did not mean to hurt her; he knew he was tipsy, and 'twas his own fault; she had been a good wife to him; she asked him for money. Then all of a sudden John drew up his form to his full height, and his chest swelled out, and he spoke in his own strong voice clearly now that he had got a topic apart from his disgrace. These were his words, a little softened into more civilised pronunciation to make them intelligible:—

'She asked I for money, she did, and what was I to gi'e her? I hadn't a got a shilling nor a sixpence, and she knew it, and knowed that I couldn't get one either till Saturday night. I gets thirteen shillings a week from Master H., and a shilling on Sundays, and I hev got five children and a wife to keep out of that—that's two shillings a week for each of us, that's just threepence halfpenny a day, look 'ee, sir.

And what victuals be I to buy wi' that, let alone beer? and a man can't do no work wi'out a quart a day, and that's fourpence, and there's my share, look 'ee, gone at onst. Wur be I to get any victuals, and wur be I to get any clothes an' boots, I should like for to know? And Jack he gets big and wants a main lot, and so did Polly, but her's gone to the work'us', wuss luck. And parson wants I to send the young 'uns to school, and pay a penny a week for 'em, and missis she wants a bit o' bacon in the house and a loaf, and what good is that of, among all we? I gets a slice of bacon twice a week, and sometimes narn. And beer—I knows I drinks beer, and more as I ought, but what's a chap to do when he's a'most shrammed wi' cold, and nar a bit o' nothin' in the pot but an old yeller swede as hard as wood? And my teeth bean't as good as 'em used to be. I knows I drinks beer, and so would anybody in my place—it makes me kinder stupid, as I don't feel nothing then. Wot's the good—I've worked this thirty year or more, since I wur big enough to go with the plough, and I've knowed they as have worked for nigh handy sixty, and wot do 'em get for it? All he'd a got wur the rheumatiz. Yer med as well drink while 'ee can. I never meaned to hurt her, and her knows it; and if it wurn't for a parcel of women a-shoving on her on, her would never a come here agen me. I knows I drinks, and what else be I to do? I can't work allus.'

'But what are you going to say in your defence—do you say she provoked you or anything?' asked the Clerk.

'No, I don't know as she provoked I. I wur provoked, though, I wur. I don't bear no malice agen she. I ain't a got nothin' more for to say.'

The magistrates retired, and the Chairman, on return-ing, said that this was a most brutal and unprovoked assault, made all the worse by the previous drinking habits of the defendant. If it had not been for the good character he bore generally speaking (here he looked towards the elder magistrate, who had evidently said a word on Smith's behalf), he would have had a month's imprisonment, or more. As it was, he was committed for a fortnight, and to pay the costs, or seven additional days; and he hoped this would be a warning to him.

The elder magistrate looked at John Smith, and saw his jaw set firmly, and his brow contract, and his heart was moved towards him.

'Cannot you get better wages than that, John?' he said. 'At the railway they would give you eighteen or twenty.'

'It's so far to walk, sir, and my legs bean't as lissom as they used to be.'

'But take the missis and live there.'

'Lodgings is too dear, sir.'

'Ah, exactly. Still I don't see how the farmers could pay you more. I'll see what can be done for you.'

Smith was led from the dock to the cell. The expenses were paid by an unknown hand; but he underwent his fortnight's imprisonment. His wife and children, with an empty larder, were obliged to go to the workhouse, where also his daughter was at the same time confined of an illegitimate child. This is no fiction, but an uncompromising picture of things as they are. Who is to blame for them?

WILTSHIRE LABOURERS

LETTER I

(To the Editor of the "Times.")

SIR,—The Wiltshire agricultural labourer is not so highly paid as those of Northumberland, nor so low as those of Dorset; but in the amount of his wages, as in intelligence and general position, he may fairly be taken as an average specimen of his class throughout a large portion of the kingdom.

As a man, he is usually strongly built, broad-shouldered, and massive in frame, but his appearance is spoilt by the clumsiness of his walk and the want of grace in his movements. Though quite as large in muscle, it is very doubtful if he possesses the strength of the seamen who may be seen lounging about the ports. There is a want of firmness, a certain disjointed style, about his limbs, and the muscles themselves have not the hardness and tension of the sailor's. The labourer's muscle is that of a cart-horse, his motions lumbering and slow. His style of walk is caused by following the plough in early childhood, when the weak limbs find it a hard labour to pull the heavy nailed boots from the thick clay soil. Ever afterwards he walks as if it were an exertion to lift his legs. His food may, perhaps, have something to do with the deadened slowness which seems to pervade everything he does—there seems a lack of vitality about him. It consists chiefly of bread and cheese, with bacon twice or thrice a week, varied with onions, and if he be a milker (on some farms) with a good 'tuck-out' at his employer's expense on Sundays. On ordinary days he dines at the fashionable hour of six or seven in the evening—that is, about that time his cottage scents the road with a powerful odour of boiled cabbage, of which he eats an immense quantity. Vegetables are his luxuries, and a large garden, therefore, is the greatest blessing he can have. He eats huge onions raw; he has no idea of flavouring his food with them, nor of making those savoury and inviting messes or vegetable soups at which the French peasantry are so clever. In Picardy I have often dined in a peasant's cottage, and thoroughly enjoyed the excellent soup he puts upon the table for his ordinary meal. To dine in an English labourer's cottage would be impossible. His bread is generally good, certainly; but his bacon is the cheapest he can buy at small second-class shops— oily, soft, wretched stuff; his vegetables are cooked in detestable style, and eaten saturated with the pot liquor. Pot liquor is a favourite soup. I have known cottagers actually apply at farmers' kitchens not only for the pot liquor in which meat has been soddened, but for the water in which potatoes have been boiled—potato liquor—and sup it up with avidity. And this is not in times of dearth or scarcity, but rather as a relish. They never buy anything but bacon; never butchers' meat. Philanthropic ladies, to my knowledge, have demonstrated over and over again even to their limited capacities that certain parts of butchers' meat can be bought just as cheap, and will make more savoury and nutritive food; and even now, with the present high price of meat, a certain proportion would be advantageous. In vain; the labourers obstinately adhere to the pig, and the pig only. When, however, an opportunity does occur the amount of food they will eat is something astonishing. Once a year, at the village club dinner, they gormandise to repletion. In one instance I knew of a man eating a plate of roast beef (and the slices are cut enormously thick at these dinners), a plate of boiled beef, then another of boiled mutton, and then a fourth of roast mutton, and a fifth of ham. He said he could not do much to the bread and cheese; but didn't he go into the pudding! I have even heard of men stuffing to the fullest extent of their powers, and then retiring from the table to take an emetic of mustard and return to a second gorging. There is scarcely any limit to their powers of absorbing beer. I have known reapers and mowers make it their boast that they could lie on their backs and never take the wooden bottle (in the shape of a small barrel) from their lips till they had drunk a gallon, and from the feats I have seen I verily believe it a fact. The beer they get is usually poor and thin, though sometimes in harvest the farmers bring out a taste of strong liquor, but not till the work is nearly over; for from this very practice of drinking enormous quantities of small beer the labourer cannot drink more than a very limited amount of good liquor without getting tipsy. This is why he so speedily gets inebriated at the alehouse While mowing and reaping many of them lay in a small cask.

They are much better clothed now than formerly. Corduroy trousers and slops are the usual style. Smock-frocks are going out of use, except for milkers and faggers. Almost every labourer has his Sunday suit, very often really good clothes, sometimes glossy black, with the regulation 'chimney-pot.' His unfortunate walk betrays him, dress how he will. Since labour has become so expensive it has become a common remark among the farmers that the labourer will go to church in broadcloth and the masters in smock-frocks. The labourer never wears gloves—that has to come with the march of the times; but he is particularly choice over his necktie. The women must dress in the fashion. A very respectable draper in an agricultural district was complaining to me the other day that the poorest class of women would have everything in the fashionable style, let it change as often as it would. In former times, if he laid in a stock of goods suited to tradesmen, and farmers' wives and daughters, if the fashion changed, or they got out of date, he could dispose of them easily to the servants. Now no such thing. The quality did not matter so much, but the style must be the style of the day—no sale for remnants. The poorest girl, who had not got two yards of flannel on her back, must have the same style of dress as the squire's daughter—Dolly Vardens, chignons, and parasols for ladies who can work all day reaping in the broiling sun of August! Gloves, kid, for hands that milk the cows!

The cottages now are infinitely better than they were. There is scarcely room for further improvement in the cottages now erected upon estates. They have three bedrooms, and every appliance and comfort compatible with their necessarily small size. It is only the cottages erected by the labourers themselves on waste plots of ground which are open to objection. Those he builds himself are, indeed, as a rule, miserable huts, disgraceful to a Christian country. I have an instance before me at this moment where a man built a cottage with two rooms and no staircase or upper apartments, and in those two rooms eight persons lived and slept—himself and wife, grown-up daughters, and children. There was not a scrap of garden attached, not enough to grow half-a-dozen onions. The refuse and sewage was flung into the road, or filtered down a ditch into the brook which supplied the part of the village with water. In another case at one time there was a cottage in which twelve persons lived. This had upper apartments, but so low was the ceiling that a tall man could stand on the floor, with his head right through the opening for the staircase, and see along the upper floor under the beds! These squatters are the curse of the community. It is among them that fever and kindred infectious diseases break out; it is among them that wretched couples are seen bent double with rheumatism and affections of the joints caused by damp. They have often been known to remain so long, generation after generation, in these wretched hovels, that at last the lord of the manor, having neglected to claim quit-rent, they can defy him, and claim them as their own property, and there they stick, eyesores and blots, the fungi of the land. The cottages erected by farmers or by landlords are now, one and all, fit and proper habitations for human beings; and I verily believe it would be impossible throughout the length and breadth of Wiltshire to find a single bad cottage on any large estate, so well and so thoroughly have the landed proprietors done their work. On all farms gardens are attached to the cottages, in many instances very large, and always sufficient to produce enough vegetables for the resident. In villages the allotment system has been greatly extended of late years, and has been found most beneficial, both to owners and tenants. As a rule the allotments are let at a rate which may be taken as £4 per annum—a sum which pays the landlord very well, and enables the labourer to remunerate himself.

In one village which came under my observation the clergyman of the parish has turned a portion of his glebe land into allotments—a most excellent and noble example, which cannot be too widely followed or too much extolled. He is thus enabled to benefit almost every one of his poor parishioners, and yet without destroying that sense of independence which is the great characteristic of a true Englishman. He has issued a book of rules and conditions under which these allotments are held, and he thus places a strong check upon drunkenness and dissolute habits, indulgence in which is a sure way to lose the portions of ground. There is scarcely an end to the benefits of the allotment system. In villages there cannot be extensive gardens, and the allotments supply their place. The extra produce above that which supplies the table and pays the rent is easily disposed of in the next town, and places many additional comforts in the labourer's reach. The refuse goes to help support and fatten the labourer's pig, which brings him in profit enough to pay the rent of his cottage, and the pig, in turn, manures the allotment. Some towns have large common lands, held under certain conditions; such are Malmesbury, with 500 acres, and Tetbury (the common land of which extends two miles), both these being arable, &c. These are not exactly in the use of labourers, but they are in the hands of a class to which the labourer often rises. Many labourers have fruit-trees in their gardens, which, in some seasons, prove very profitable. In the present year, to my knowledge, a labourer sold £4 worth of apples; and another made £3, 10s. off the produce of one pear-tree, pears being scarce.

To come at last to the difficult question of wages. In Wiltshire there has been no extended strike, and very few meetings upon the subject, for the simple reason that the agitators can gain no hold upon a county where, as a mass, the labourers are well paid. The common day-labourer receives 10s., 11s., and 12s. a week, according to the state of supply and demand for labour in various districts; and, if he milks, 1s. more, making 13s. a week, now common wages. These figures are rather below the mark; I could give instances of much higher pay. To give a good idea of the wages paid I will take the case of a hill farmer (arable, Marlborough Downs), who paid this last summer during harvest 18s. per week per man. His reapers often earned 10s. a day—enough to pay their year's rent in a week. These men lived in cottages on the farm, with three bedrooms each, and some larger, with every modern appliance, each having a garden of a quarter of an acre attached and close at hand, for which cottage and garden they paid 1s. per week rent. The whole of these cottages were insured by the farmer himself, their furniture, &c., in one lump, and the insurance policy cost him, as nearly as possible, 1s. 3d. per cottage per year. For this he deducted 1s. per year each from their wages. None of the men would have insured unless he had insisted upon doing it for them. These men had from six to eight quarts of beer per man (over and above their 18s. a week) during harvest every day. In spring and autumn their wages are much increased by piece-work, hoeing, &c. In winter the farmer draws their coal for them in his waggons, a distance of eight miles from the nearest wharf, enabling them to get it at cost price. This is no slight advantage, for, at the present high price of coal, it is sold, delivered in the villages, at 2s. per cwt. Many who cannot afford it in the week buy a quarter of a cwt. on Saturday night, to cook their Sunday's dinner with, for 6d. This is at the rate of £2 per ton. Another gentleman, a large steam cultivator in the Vale, whose name is often before the public, informs me that his books show that he paid £100 in one year in cash to one cottage for labour, showing the advantage the labourer possesses over the mechanic, since his wife and child can add to his income. Many farmers pay £50 and £60 a year for beer drunk by their labourers—a serious addition to their wages. The railway companies and others who employ mechanics do not allow them any beer. The allowance of a good cottage and a quarter of an acre of garden for 1s. per week is not singular. Many who were at the Autumn Manoeuvres of the present year may remember having a handsome row of houses, rather than cottages, pointed out to them as inhabited by labourers at 1s. per week. In the immediate neighbourhood of large manufacturing towns 1s. 6d. a week is sometimes paid; but then these cottages would in such positions readily let to mechanics for 3s., 4s., and even 5s. per week. There was a great outcry when the Duke of Marlborough issued an order that the cottages on his estate should in future only be let to such men as worked upon the farms where those cottages were situated. In reality this was the very greatest blessing the Duke could have conferred upon the agricultural labourer; for it ensured him a good cottage at a nearly nominal rent and close to his work; whereas in many instances previously the cottages on the farms had been let at a high rate to the mechanics, and the labourer had to walk miles before he got to his labour. Cottages are not erected by landowners or by farmers as paying speculations. It is well known that the condition of things prevents the agricultural labourer from being able to pay a sufficient rent to be a fair percentage upon the sum expended. In one instance a landlord has built some cottages for his tenant, the tenant paying a certain amount of interest on the sum invested by the landlord. Now, although this is a matter of arrangement, and not of speculation—that is, although the interest paid by the tenant is a low percentage upon the money laid out, yet the rent paid by the labourers inhabiting these cottages to the tenant does not reimburse him when he pays his landlord as interest—not by a considerable margin. But then he has the advantage of his labourers close to his work, always ready at hand.

Over and above the actual cash wages of the labourer, which are now very good, must be reckoned his cottage and garden, and often a small orchard, at a nominal rent, his beer at his master's expense, piece-work, gleaning after harvest, &c., which alter his real position very materially. In Gloucestershire, on the Cotswolds, the best-paid labourers are the shepherds, for in that great sheep-country much trust is reposed in them. At the annual auctions of shearlings which are held upon the large farms a purse is made for the shepherd of the flock, into which every one who attends is expected to drop a shilling, often producing £5. The shepherds on the Wiltshire Downs are also well paid, especially in lambing-time, when the greatest watchfulness and care are required. It has been stated that the labourer has no chance of rising from his position. This is sheer cant. He has very good opportunities of rising, and often does rise, to my knowledge. At this present moment I could mention a person who has risen from a position scarcely equal to that of a labourer, not only to have a farm himself, but to place his sons in farms. Another has just entered on a farm; and several more are on the high-road to that desirable consummation. If a labourer possesses any amount of intelligence he becomes a head-carter or head-fagger, as the case may be; and from that to be assistant or under-bailiff, and finally bailiff. As a bailiff he has every opportunity to learn the working of a farm, and is often placed in entire charge of a farm at a distance from his employer's residence. In time he establishes a reputation as a practical man, and being in receipt of good wages, with very little expenditure, saves some money. He has now little difficulty in obtaining the promise of a farm, and with this can readily take up money. With average care he is a made man. Others rise from petty trading, petty dealing in pigs and calves, till they save sufficient to rent a small farm, and make the basis of larger dealing operations. I question very much whether a clerk in a firm would not find it much more difficult, as requiring larger capital, to raise himself to a level with his employer than an agricultural labourer does to the level of a farmer.

Many labourers now wander far and wide as navvies, &c., and perhaps when these return home, as most of them do, to agricultural labour, they are the most useful and intelligent of their class, from a readiness they possess to turn their hand to anything. I know one at this moment who makes a large addition to his ordinary wages by brewing for the small inns, and very good liquor he brews, too. They pick up a large amount of practical knowledge.

The agricultural women are certainly not handsome; I know no peasantry so entirely uninviting. Occasionally there is a girl whose nut-brown complexion and sloe-black eyes are pretty, but their features are very rarely good, and they get plain quickly, so soon as the first flush of youth is past. Many have really good hair in abundance, glossy and rich, perhaps from its exposure to the fresh air. But on Sundays they plaster it with strong-smelling

pomade and hair-oil, which scents the air for yards most
unpleasantly. As a rule, it may safely be laid down that the
agricultural women are moral, far more so than those of
the town. Rough and rude jokes and language are, indeed,
too common; but that is all. No evil comes of it. The fairs
are the chief cause of immorality. Many an honest, hard-
working servant-girl owes her ruin to these fatal mops and
fairs, when liquor to which she is unaccustomed overcomes her. Yet it seems cruel to take from them the one
day or two of the year on which they can enjoy themselves
fairly in their own fashion. The spread of friendly
societies, patronised by the gentry and clergy, with their
annual festivities, is a remedy which is gradually supply-
ing them with safe, and yet congenial, amusement. In
what may be termed lesser morals I cannot accord either
them or the men the same phrase. They are too ungrateful
for the many great benefits which are bountifully supplied
them—the brandy, the soup, and fresh meat readily extended without stint from the farmer's home in sickness to
the cottage are too quickly forgotten. They who were
most benefited are often the first to most loudly complain
and to backbite. Never once in all my observation have I
heard a labouring man or woman make a grateful remark;
and yet I can confidently say that there is no class of
persons in England who receive so many attentions and
benefits from their superiors as the agricultural labourers.
Stories are rife of their even refusing to work at disastrous
fires because beer was not immediately forthcoming. I
trust this is not true; but it is too much in character. No
term is too strong in condemnation for those persons who
endeavour to arouse an agitation among a class of people
so short-sighted and so ready to turn against their own
benefactors and their own interest. I am credibly informed

that one of these agitators, immediately after the Bishop of Gloucester's unfortunate but harmlessly intended speech at the Gloucester Agricultural Society's dinner—one of these agitators mounted a platform at a village meeting and in plain language incited and advised the labourers to duck the farmers! The agricultural women either go out to field-work or become indoor servants. In harvest they hay-make—chiefly light work, as raking—and reap, which is much harder labour; but then, while reaping they work their own time, as it is done by the piece. Significantly enough, they make longer hours while reaping. They are notoriously late to arrive, and eager to return home, on the hay-field. The children help both in haymaking and reaping. In spring and autumn they hoe and do other piece-work. On pasture farms they beat clots or pick up stones out of the way of the mowers' scythes. Occasionally, but rarely now, they milk. In winter they wear gaiters, which give the ankles a most ungainly appearance. Those who go out to service get very low wages at first from their extreme awkwardness, but generally quickly rise. As dairymaids they get very good wages indeed. Dairymaids are scarce and valuable. A dairymaid who can be trusted to take charge of a dairy will sometimes get £20 besides her board (liberal) and sundry perquisites. These often save money, marry bailiffs, and help their husbands to start a farm.

In the education provided for children Wiltshire compares favourably with other counties. Long before the passing of the recent Act in reference to education the clergy had established schools in almost every parish, and their exertions have enabled the greater number of places to come up to the standard required by the Act, without the assistance of a School Board. The great difficulty is the distance children have to walk to school, from the sparseness of population and the number of outlying hamlets. This difficulty is felt equally by the farmers, who, in the majority of cases, find themselves situated far from a good school. In only one place has anything like a cry for education arisen, and that is on the extreme northern edge of the county. The Vice-Chairman of the Swindon Chamber of Agriculture recently stated that only one-half of the entire population of Inglesham could read and write. It subsequently appeared that the parish of Inglesham was very sparsely populated, and that a variety of circumstances had prevented vigorous efforts being made. The children, however, could attend schools in adjoining parishes, not farther than two miles, a distance which they frequently walk in other parts of the country.

Those who are so ready to cast every blame upon the farmer, and to represent him as eating up the earnings of his men and enriching himself with their ill-paid labour, should remember that farming, as a rule, is carried on with a large amount of borrowed capital. In these days, when £6 an acre has been expended in growing roots for sheep, when the slightest derangement of calculation in the price of wool, meat, or corn, or the loss of a crop, seriously interferes with a fair return for capital invested, the farmer has to sail extremely close to the wind, and only a little more would find his canvas shaking. It was only recently that the cashier of the principal bank of an agricultural county, after an unprosperous year, declared that such another season would make almost every farmer insolvent. Under these circumstances it is really to be wondered at that they have done as much as they have for the labourer in the last few years, finding him with better cottages, better wages, better education, and affording him better opportunities of rising in the social scale.—I am, Sir, faithfully yours,

RICHARD JEFFERIES.

Coate Farm, Swindon, Nov. 12, 1872

Lord Shaftesbury, in the *Times*, Dec. 6th, says:—

'It is our duty and our interest to elevate the present condition of the labourer, and to enable him to assert and enjoy every one of his rights. But I must agree with Mr. Jefferies that, even under the actual system of things, numerous instances have occurred of a rise in the social scale as the result of temperance, good conduct, and economy. He has furnished some examples. I will give only one from my own estate:—'T. M. was for many years shepherd to Farmer P—; he bought with his savings a small leasehold property at — for £170, and he had accumulated £100 besides. He had brought up a son and three daughters, and his son now occupies the leasehold.' This is the statement as given to me in writing.'

LETTER II

(To the Editor of the "Times.")

SIR,—I did not intend to make any reply to the numerous attacks made upon my letter published in the *Times* of the 14th inst., but the statements made by 'The Son of a Wiltshire Labourer' are such as I feel bound to resent on the part of the farmers of this county.

He says he wishes the landed proprietors would take as much care to provide cottages for their labourers as I represent them as doing. I repeat what I said, that the cottages on large estates are now, one and all, fit for habitations for human beings. The Duke of Marlborough is a large proprietor of cottages in this neighbourhood, and his plan has been, whenever a cottage did not appear sufficiently commodious, to throw two into one. The owner of the largest estate near Swindon has been engaged for many years past in removing the old thatched mud hovels, and replacing them with substantial, roomy, and slate-roofed buildings. Farmers are invariably anxious to have good cottages. There is a reluctance to destroy the existing ones, both from the inconvenience and the uncertainty sometimes of others being erected. Often, too, the poor have the strongest attachment to the cabin in which they were born and bred, and would strongly resent its destruction, though obviously for their good. Farmers never build bad cottages now. When a tenement falls in, either from decay or the death of the tenant, the cottage which is erected on its site is invariably a good one. A row of splendid cottages has recently been erected at Wanborough. They are very large, with extensive gardens attached. Some even begin to complain that the cottages now erected are in a sense 'too good' for the purpose. The system of three bedrooms is undoubtedly the best from a sanitary point of view, but it is a question whether the widespread belief in that system, and that system alone, has not actually retarded the erection of reasonably good buildings. It is that third bedroom which just prevents the investment of building a cottage from paying a remunerative percentage on the capital expended. Two bedrooms are easily made—the third puzzles the builder where to put it with due regard to economy. Nor is a third bedroom always required. Out of ten families perhaps only two require a third bedroom; in this way there is a large waste in erecting a row. It has been suggested that a row should consist of so many cottages with two bedrooms only for families who do not want more, and at each end a building with three bedrooms for larger families. In one instance two cottages were ordered to be erected on an estate, the estimate for which was £640; these when completed might have let for £10 per annum, or 1¾ per cent. on the capital invested! The plans for these cottages had so many dormer windows, porches, intricacies of design in variegated tiles, &c., that the contractor gave it up as a bad job. I mention this to show that the tendency to build good cottages has gone even beyond what was really required, and ornamentation is added to utility.

Then it is further stated that the labourer cannot build cottages. I could name a lane at this moment the cottages in which were one and all built by labourers; and there are half-a-dozen in this village which were erected by regular farm labourers. The majority of these are, as I said before, wretched hovels, but there are two or three which demonstrate that the labourer, if he is a thrifty man, earns quite sufficient to enable him to erect a reasonably good building. The worst hovel I ever saw (it was mentioned in my letter of the 14th) was built by a man who is notorious for his drinking habits. Some forty years ago, when wages were much lower than they are now, two labourers, to my knowledge, took possession of a strip of waste land by the roadside, and built themselves cottages. One of these was a very fair building; the other would certainly be condemned now-a-days. The lord of the manor claimed these; and the difficulty was thus adjusted:—The builders were to receive the value of their tenements from the lord of the manor, and were to remain permanent tenants for life on payment of a small percentage, interest upon the purchase-money, as quit-rent. On their deaths the cottages were to become the property of the lord of the manor. One man received £40 for his cottage, the other £20, which sums forty years ago represented relatively a far higher value than now, and demonstrate conclusively that the labourer, if he is a steady, hard-working man, can build a cottage. Another cottage I know of, built by a farm labourer, is really a very creditable building—good walls, floors, stair-case, sashes, doors; it stands high, and appears very com-fortable, and even pleasant, in summer, for they are a thrifty family, and can even display flower-pots in the window. Other cottages have been built or largely added to in my memory by labourers. On these occasions they readily obtain help from the farmers. One lends his team and waggons to draw the stones; another supplies wood for nothing; but of late I must admit there has been some reluctance to assist in this way (unless for repairs) because it was so often found that the buildings thus erected were not fit habitations. The Boards of Guardians often find a difficulty from the limited ownership of some of the labourers, who apply for relief, of their cottages. Perhaps they have not paid quit-rent for a year or two; but still they cannot sell, and yet it seems unjust to the ratepayers to assist a man who has a tenement which he at least calls his own, and from which he cannot be ejected. I know a labourer at this moment living in a cottage originally built by his father, and added to by himself by the assistance of the neighbouring farmers. This man has been greatly as-sisted by one farmer in particular, who advanced him money by which he purchased a horse and cart, and was enabled to do a quantity of hauling, flint-carting for the waywardens, and occasionally to earn money by assisting to carry a farmer's harvest. He rents a large piece of arable land, and ought to be comparatively well off.

'The Son of a Wiltshire Labourer' complains that the farmers or proprietors do not make sufficient efforts to supply the cottages with water. The lord of the manor and the tenant of the largest farms in this immediate neighbourhood have but just sunk a well for their cottages; previously they had got their supply from a pump in an adjacent farmyard thrown open by the proprietor to all the village.

It is the labourer himself who will not rise. In a village with which I am acquainted great efforts have been made by a farmer and a gentleman living near to provide proper school instruction for the children. One labourer was asked why he did not send his children to school. He replied, 'Because he could not afford it.' 'But,' said the farmer, 'it is only threepence altogether.' 'Oh, no; he could not afford it.' The farmer explained to him that the object was to avoid a School Board, which, in other places, had the power to fine for not sending children to school. 'No, he could not afford it.' The farmer's books show that this labourer, his wife, and two children received 28s. 6d. per week, his cottage rent free, and a very large garden at a low rent. Yet he could not afford the 3d. a week which would enable his children ultimately to take a better position in the world! The same farmer, who is a liberal and large-minded man, has endeavoured, without success, to introduce the practice of paying in cash instead of beer, and also the system of payment for overtime. The men say no, they would rather not. 'In wet weather,' they say, 'we do no work, but you pay us; and if we work a little later in harvest, it only makes it fair.' They would not take money instead of beer. In another case which came under my personal observation in the middle of last summer, a farmer announced his intention of paying in cash instead of allowing beer. In the very press of the haymaking, with acres upon acres of grass spoiling, his men, one and all, struck work because he would not give them beer, and went over to a neighbour's field adjacent and worked for him for nothing but their share in the beer. If labourers work longer hours in harvest (corn), it is because it is piece-work, and they thereby make more money. I contend that the payment in kind, the beer, the gleanings, the piece-work, the low and nominal cottage rent, the allotment ground and produce, and the pig (not restricted to one pig in a year), may fairly be taken as an addition to their wages. I am informed that in one parish the cottage rents vary from 10d. to 1s. 2d. per week; nearly all have gardens, and all may have allotments up to a quarter of an acre each at 3d. per lug, or 40s. per acre. I am also informed of a labourer renting a cottage and garden at 1s. per week, the fruit-trees in whose garden produced this year three sacks of damsons, which he sold at 1s. 6d. per gallon, or £6. 18s. I know of a case in which a labourer—an earnest, intelligent, hard-working man—makes £2 a week on an average all the year round. But then he works only at piece-work, going from farm to farm, and this is, of course, an exceptional case. The old men, worn out with age and infirmity, are kept on year after year by many farmers out of charity, rather than let them go to the workhouse, though totally useless and a dead loss, especially as occupying valuable cottage-room. There is a society, the annual meetings of which are held at Chippenham, and which is supported by the clergy, gentry, and farmers generally of North Wilts, for the object of promoting steady habits among the labourers and rewarding cases of long and deserving services. There is also a friendly society on the best and most reliable basis, supported by the gentry, and introduced as far as possible into villages. The labourers on the Great Western Railway works at Swindon earn from 15s. a week upwards, according as they approach to skilled workmen. Attracted by these wages, most of the young men of the neighbourhood try the factory, but, usually, after a short period return to farm-work, the result of their experience being that they are better off as agricultural labourers. Lodgings in the town close to the factory are very expensive, and food in proportion; consequently they have to walk long distances to their labour—some from Wanborough, five miles; Wroughton, three and a half miles; Purton, four miles; and even Wootton Bassett, six miles, which twice a day is a day's work in itself. Add to this the temptations to spend money in towns, and the severe labour, and the man finds himself better off with his quiet cottage and garden on a farm at 12s. a week, and 1s. for milking, with beer, and a meal on Sundays. The skilled mechanics, who earn 36s. to £2 per week, rent houses in the town at 6s. to 8s.; and in one case I knew of 12s. per week paid by a lodger for two rooms. These prices cannot be paid out of the mechanic's wage; consequently he sub-lets, or takes lodgers, and sometimes these sub-let, and the result is an overcrowding worse than that of the agricultural cottages, around which there is at least fresh air and plenty of light (nearly as important), which are denied in a town. The factory labourer and the mechanic are liable to instant dismissal. The agricultural labourers (half of them at least) are hired by the year or half-year, and cannot be summarily sent along unless for misconduct. Wages have recently been increased by the farmers of Wiltshire voluntarily and without pressure from threatened strikes. It is often those who receive the highest wages who are the first to come to the parish for relief. It is not uncommon for mechanics and others to go for relief where it is discovered that they are in receipt of sick pay from the yard club, and sometimes from two friendly societies, making 18s. a week. A manufacturing gentleman informed me that the very men whom he had been paying £8 a week to were the first to apply for relief when distress came and the mills stopped. It is not low wages, then, which causes improvident habits. The only result of deporting agricultural labourers to different counties is to equalise the wages paid all over England. This union-assisted emigration affords the improvident labourer a good opportunity of transporting himself to a distant county, and leaving deeply in debt with the tradesmen with whom he has long dealt. I am informed that this is commonly the case with emigrating labourers. A significant fact is noted in the leader of the *Labour News* of the 16th of November; the return of certain emigrants from America is announced as 'indicative that higher quotations are not always representative of greater positive advantages.' The agricultural labourer found that out when he returned from the factory at 15s. per week to farm labour at 12s. I am positive that the morality of the country compares favourably with that of the town. I was particularly struck with this fact on a visit to the Black Country. One of the worst parishes for immorality in Wiltshire is one where glovemaking is carried on; singularly enough, manufactures and immorality seem to go together. 'The Son of a Labourer' says that all the advantages the labourer does possess are owing to the exertions of the clergy; pray who support the clergy but the farmers?

I think that the facts I have mentioned sufficiently demonstrate that the farmers and the landlords of Wiltshire have done their duty, and more than their mere duty, towards the labourers; and only a little investigation will show that at present it is out of their power to do more. Take the case of a farmer entering a dairy-farm of, say, 250 acres, and calculate his immediate outgoings—say fifty cows at £20, £1,000; two horses at £25, £50; waggons, carts, implements, £100; labour, three men at 12s. per week, £94; harvest labour, £20; dairymaid £10; tithe, taxes, rates, &c., £100; rent, £2 per acre, £500. Total, £1874. In other words (exclusive of the capital invested in stock), the outgoings amount to £724 per annum; against which put—fifty cows' milk, &c., at £10 per head, £500; fifty calves, £100; fifty tons of hay at £3, 10s., £175. Total income, £775; balance in hand, £51. Then comes the village school subscription; sometimes a church rate (legally voluntary, but morally binding), &c.

So that, in hard figures (all these are below the mark, if anything), there is positively nothing left for the farmer but a house and garden free. How, then, is money made? By good judgment in crops, in stock, by lucky accidents. On a dairy-farm the returns begin immediately; on an arable one there is half a year at least to wait. The care, the judgment, required to be exercised is something astonishing, and a farmer is said to be all his life learning his trade. If sheep are dear and pay well, the farmer plants roots; then, perhaps, after a heavy expenditure for manure, for labour, and seed, there comes the fly, or a drought, and his capital is sunk. On the other hand, if the season be good, roots are cheap and over-plentiful, and where is his profit then? He works like a labourer himself in all weathers and at all times; he has the responsibility and the loss, yet he is expected to find the labourer, not only good cottages, allotments, schooling, good wages, but Heaven knows what besides. Supposing the £1874 (on the dairy-farm) be borrowed capital for which he must pay at least 4 per cent.—and few, indeed, are there who get money at that price—it is obvious how hard he must personally work, how hard, too, he must live, to make both ends meet. And it speaks well for his energy and thrift that I heard a bank director not long since remark that he had noticed, after all, with every drawback, the tenant farmers had made as a rule more money in proportion than their landlords. A harder-working class of men does not exist than the Wilt-shire farmers.

Only a few days ago I saw in your valuable paper a list, nearly a column long, of the millionaires who had died in the last ten years. It would be interesting to know how much they had spent for the benefit of the agricultural labourer. Yet no one attacks them. They pay no poor-rates, no local taxation, or nothing in proportion. The farmer pays the poor-rate which supports the labourer in disease, accident, and old age; the highway rates on which the millionaire's carriage rolls; and very soon the turnpike trusts will fall in, and the farmers—*i.e.*, the land—will have to support the imperial roads also. With all these heavy burdens on his back, having to compete against the world, he has yet no right to compensation for his invested capital if he is ordered to quit. Without some equalisation of local taxation—as I have shown, the local taxes often make another rent almost—without a recognised tenant-right, not revolutionary, but for unexhausted improve-ments, better security, so that he can freely invest capital, the farmer cannot—I reiterate it, he cannot—do more than he has done for the labourer. He would then employ more skilled labour, and wages would be better. And, after all that he does for them, he dares not find fault, or he may find his ricks blazing away—thanks to the teaching of the agitators that the farmers are tyrants, and, by inference, that to injure them is meritorious. There is a poster in Swindon now offering £20 reward for the discovery of the person who maliciously set fire to a rick of hay in Lord Bolingbroke's park at Lydiard.

If any farmers are hard upon their men, it is those who have themselves been labourers and have risen to be employers of labour. These very often thoroughly understand the art of getting the value of a man's wage out of him. I deliberately affirm that the true farmers, one and all, are in favour of that maxim of a well-known and respected agriculturist of our county—'A fair day's wage for a fair day's work.'

I fear the farmers of Wiltshire would be only too happy to ride thorough-breds to the hunt, and see their daughters driving phaetons, as they are accused of doing; but I also fear that very, very few enjoy that privilege. Most farmers, it is true, do keep some kind of vehicle; it is necessary when their great distance from a town is considered, and the keep of a horse or two comes to nothing on a large farm. It is customary for them to drive their wives or daughters once a week on market-days into the nearest town. If here and there an energetic man succeeds in making money, and is able to send his son to a university, all honour to him. I hope the farmers will send their sons to universities; the spread of education in their class will be of as much advantage to the community as among the labouring population, for it will lead to the more general application of science to the land and a higher amount of production. If the labourer attempted to rise he would be praised; why not the farmer?

It is simply an unjustifiable libel on the entire class to accuse them of wilful extravagance. I deliberately affirm that the majority of farmers in Wiltshire are exactly the reverse; that, while they practise a generous hospitality to a friend or a stranger, they are decidedly saving and frugal rather than extravagant, and they are compelled to be so by the condition of their finances. To prove that their efforts are for the good of the community I need only allude to the work of the late Mr. Stratton, so crowned with success in improving the breed of cattle—a work in the sister county of Gloucester so ably carried on at this present moment by Mr. Edward Bowly, and by Mr. Lane and Mr. Garne in the noted Cotswold sheep. The breeds produced by these gentlemen have in a manner impregnated the whole world, imported as they have been to America and Australia. It was once ably said that the readings of the English Bible Sunday after Sunday in our churches had preserved our language pure for centuries; and, in the same way, I do verily believe that the English (not the Wiltshire only, but the English) farmer as an institution, with his upright, untainted ideas of honour, honesty, and morality, has preserved the tone of society from that corruption which has so miserably degraded France—so much so that Dumas recently scientifically predicted that France was *en route à prostitution générale*. Just in the same way his splendid constitution as a man recruits the exhausted, pale, nervous race who dwell in cities, and prevents the Englishman from physically degenerating.—I am, Sir, faithfully yours,

RICHARD JEFFERIES

Coate Farm, Swindon, November 12, 1872.

The Allotment System

(To the Editor of the "Times.")

SIR,—Many gentlemen having written to me for further information upon the system of glebe allotments for labourers mentioned in my letter to the *Times* of November 14, it has occurred to me that the following facts may be interesting:—

The glebe alluded to was that of Lyddington, near Swindon, and the plan was originated by the late incumbent, Mr. May, but carried out into a complete system by the present much-respected rector, the Rev. H. Munn. The land itself is situated not more than 300 yards from the village of Lyddington, by the side of a good turnpike-road, and is traversed by two roads giving easy access to every allotment. Each plot of ground is divided from the next by a narrow green path: no hedges or mounds are permitted, and the field itself is enclosed without a hedge to harbour birds. The soil is a rich dark loam, yielding good crops, with very little manure, and the surface is level. There are sixty-three tenants occupying plots varying in size, according to circumstances, from 48 'lug' downwards—25, 30, 16, &c. A 'lug' is a provincialism for perch. The rent is 5d. per 'lug' or perch, and each occupier on becoming a tenant receives a card on which the following rules are printed in large type:—

'Lyddington Garden Allotments'

'RULES AND REGULATIONS'

'1. The land shall be cultivated by the spade only, and proper attention shall be paid to its cultivation.

'2. No allotment, or any part thereof, shall be under-let or exchanged.

'3. The rent shall be due on the 1st of September in each year, and shall be paid before the crop is taken off the ground.

'4. All tenants shall maintain a character for morality and sobriety, and shall not frequent a public-house on the Sabbath day.

'5. If any tenant fail to pay his rent or to perform any of the foregoing conditions he shall immediately forfeit his allotment, with his crop upon the same, and the landlord or his agent shall take possession and enforce payment of the rent due by sale of the crop or otherwise, as in arrears of rent.

'All the tenants are earnestly requested to attend regularly at the House of God during the times of Divine Service, with their families, to the best of their abilities.'

The object of Rule 2 is to enable the landlord to retain a certain amount of influence over the tenant, to bring him in immediate contact with the tenant, and to keep the land itself under his control. Many occupiers endeavour to under-let their allotments, which, if permitted, would entirely defeat the main object of the landlord, besides complicating the already great labour of collecting the rents, &c.

Rule 3 prevents the produce of the allotment going to pay the public-house score; while the date on which the rent falls due is so adjusted as to enable the occupier to receive his money for harvest-work before paying it.

Rule 4 places a great restraint upon drunkenness and dissolute habits. Last year the Rev. H. Munn addressed a private circular to his tenants, in which he says:—

'Sad reports have been brought to me lately of the conduct of some in the parish, and among them, I am sorry to say, are tenants of the Allotment Gardens. Such conduct is contrary to the rules on which the allotments are held, and also contrary to the intentions of my predecessor in letting them out to the parishioners. They are intended to improve the condition of the labourers and their families, giving them employment in the summer evenings, increasing their supply of food, and withdrawing them from the influence of the public-house. But when drinking habits are indulged all these benefits are lost, and the allotments, which were intended to do the labourer good, only increase his means of obtaining intoxicating drinks.'

The landlord can, of course, exercise his discretion in enforcing Rule 5—can allow time for payment, and in certain cases of misfortune, such as the failure of the potato crop, remit it entirely. But this power must be sparingly used, otherwise every one would endeavour to find excuses for non-fulfilment of the contract.

The extent of the allotment is written on the back of the card of rules, with the name of the tenant, thus:—'D. Hancock.—Lot 1, Lug 15; rent 6s. 3d.;' and each payment is receipted underneath, with the date and initials of the landlord.

The present landlord has in no case disturbed or re-

moved the tenants received by his predecessor, but where
land has fallen in he has endeavoured to arrange the extent
of the new allotments made to suit the requirements of
families, and to allow of a sufficient crop of potatoes being
grown for one season on one half of the allotment, while
the other half bears different vegetables, and *vice versâ* for
the next season, being the same thing as a rotation of
crops.

The field has recently been drained at the joint cost of
landlord and tenant. The Rev. H. Munn provided the
drain-pipes, and the occupiers paid for the labour, which
latter came to £8, the amount being proportioned according to the size of each allotment. The highest amount paid
by any one tenant was, I believe, £1 (for 48 'lug'), others
going down to 1s.

The rent at 5d. per 'lug' or perch comes to £3, 6s. 8d. per
acre, an amount which bears a proper relation to the rent of
arable farming land, when the labour of collecting so
many small sums and other circumstances are taken into
consideration. The moral effect of the arrangement has
been incalculable—as one old woman pertinently remarked, 'We needn't steal now, sir.' In the olden times the
farmers' gardens were constantly subject to depredations.
The ordinary rate at which gardens are let in the neighbourhood is 6d. per 'lug.' At Swindon, the nearest town
(12,000 inhabitants), there are large allotment fields let at
1s. 6d. per 'lug,' or £12 per acre, and eagerly caught up at
that price. These allotments are rented by every class,
from labourers and mechanics to well-to-do tradesmen.

The very first desire of every agricultural labourer's
heart is a garden, and so strong is the feeling that I have
known men apply for permission to cultivate the vacant
space between the large double mounds of the hedges on

some pasture farms, and work hard at it despite the roots of the bushes and the thefts of the rooks.

The facts mentioned above only add one more to the numberless ways in which the noble clergy of the Church of England have been silently labouring for the good of the people committed to their care for years before the agitators bestowed one thought on the agricultural poor.—I am, Sir, faithfully yours,

RICHARD JEFFERIES

Coate Farm, Swindon

(*Published in the "Times," Nov. 23, 1872*)

A True Tale of the Wiltshire Labourer

'Now then—hold fast there—mind the furrow, Tim.' The man who was loading prepared himself for the shock, and the waggon safely jolted over the furrow, and on between the wakes of light-brown hay, crackling to the touch as if it would catch fire in the brilliant sunshine. The pitchers, one on each side, stuck their prongs into the wakes and sent up great 'pitches,' clearing the ground rapidly, through emulation, for it was a point of honour to keep pace with each other. Tim, the old man who had led the horses, resumed his rake in the rear among the women, who instantly began teasing the poor wretch.

'Tim, she's allus in the way,' said one, purposely hitching her rake in his. 'Thur—get away.'

'I shan't,' said Tim, surly as crabbed age and incessant banter under a hot sun could make him. 'Now—mind, thee's break th' rake.'

They both pulled as hard as they dared—each expecting the other to give way, for the master was in sight, on horseback, by the rick, and a rake broken wantonly would bring a sharp reprimand.

'Go it, Sal!' cried the loader on the waggon hoarsely, half choked with hay dust. 'Pull away!'

'Pull, Tim!' cried one of the pitchers.

'Ha! ha!' laughed two or three more women, closing round as the girl gave a tug which nearly upset Tim and broke half-a-dozen teeth out of his rake.

'Darn thee!' growled the old fellow. The youngest of the girls at the same moment gave him a push under the arm with the end of her rake-handle. It was the last straw which broke the back of Tim's temper. Swearing, he dropped the rake and seized a prong, and hobbled after the girl, who danced away half in delight and half in terror.

'I'll job this into thee—darn thee—if I can come near thee, thee hussy!'

The 'hussy' let him come near, and danced away again gracefully. She was at once the most handsome and most impudent of his tormentors. There's no saying whether the old man, roused as he was and incensed beyond control, might not really have 'jobbed,' *i.e.*, stabbed, his prong at her, had not one of the pitchers left his wake and rushed on him.

'My eye!' shouted the loader, 'Absalom's at 'un!'

Absalom took Tim by the shoulders and hurled him on the ground pretty heavily. Flinging the prong twenty yards away, he threatened to knock his head off if he didn't let Madge alone. Old Tim slowly got up and went off after his tool, growling to himself, while Madge clung hold of Absalom's arm, who, turning round, kissed her. The other women looked jealously on as she followed him back to his wake, and kept close to him at his work.

Madge was tall and slenderly made. Her limbs were more delicately proportioned than is usual among women accustomed to manual labour from childhood. The rosy glow of health lit up her brown but clear cheek, free from freckles and sunspots. Her eyes, black as sloes, were fringed with long dark eyelashes which gave their glances an *espiègle* expression. They were very wicked-looking eyes, full of fun and mischief. Her dress, open at the throat, displayed a faultless neck, but slightly sun-browned. Her curly dark-brown hair escaped in ringlets down her back. A lovely nut-brown maid!

Soft glances passed rapidly between Madge and Absalom, as she raked behind him. They did not escape the jealous notice of the other women. It was the last day of the hay-harvest—it was 'hay home' that night.

Harvest is a time of freedom, but the last day resembles the ancient Saturnalia, or rather perhaps the vine season in Italy, when the grape-gatherers indulged their rude wit on every one who came near. Raillery and banter poured incessantly on Madge and Absalom, who replied with equal freedom.

'Grin away,' shouted Absalom at last, half pleased, half irritated, as he stuck his prong in the ground, and seizing Madge, kissed her before them all. 'Thur—I bean't ashamed on her!'

'Ha! ha! ha! Hoorah!' shouted the men. Madge slipped away towards the rear, blushing scarlet. So absorbed had they been as not to notice the approach of another waggon coming in the opposite direction, which was now alongside. Seeing the kiss and hearing the laugh, one of the men, following it, shouted in a stentorian voice, for which he was renowned—

'Darn my buttons if I won't have one of they!'

In an instant he was over the wake and caught Madge in his arms. But she struggled and cried. Absalom was there in a moment.

'Go it, Roaring Billy!' shouted the followers of the other waggon. But Absalom shook him free, and the girl darted away. The two men stood fronting each other. Absalom was angry. Billy had had a trifle too much beer. A quarrel was imminent, and fists were doubled, when the pitchers rushed up and separated them.

The last pitch was now flung up, and the women began to decorate the horses and the waggons with green boughs.

'Come on, Madge,' said Absalom, 'we'll ride whoam;' and despite of much feminine shyness and many objections, and after much trouble and blushing and rude jokes about legs, Madge was hoisted up, and Absalom followed her. To the rick-yard they rode in triumph among green boughs, and to the rude chorus of a song.

At seven that evening the whole gang were collected in the farmer's great kitchen. A huge room it was, paved with stone flags, the walls whitewashed, and the ceiling being the roof itself, whose black beams were festooned with cobwebs. Three or four tables had been arranged in a row, and there was a strong smell of 'dinner' from smoking joints. Absalom came in last. He had spent some time in adorning himself in a white clean slop and new corduroys, with a gay necktie and his grandfather's watch. His face shone from a recent wash. It was an open countenance, which unconsciously prepossessed one in his favour. Light-blue or grey eyes, which looked you straight in the face, were over-shadowed with rather thick eyebrows. His forehead was well proportioned, and crowned with a mass of curling yellow hair. A profusion of whiskers hid his chin, which perhaps in its shape indicated a character too easy and yielding. His shoulders were broad; his appearance one of great strength. But his mouth had a sensual look. Absalom pushed in and out by Madge.

'What didst thee have to eat?' asked a crony of his afterwards.

'Aw,' said Absalom, fetching a sigh at the remembrance of the good things. 'Fust I had a plate of rus beef, then a plate of boiled beef; then I had one of boiled mutton, and next one of roast mutton; last, bacon. I found I couldn't git on at all wi' th' pudding, but when the cheese and th' salad came, didn't I pitch into that!'

Absalom's love did not spoil his appetite.

Soon as the dishes were removed pipes were brought out and tankards sent on their rounds. By this time poor old Tim's weak brains were muddled, and he was discovered leaning back against the wall and mumbling out the tag-end of an old song:—

> '*On' Humphry wi' his flail,*
> *But Kitty she wur the charming ma-aid*
> *To carry th' milking pa-ail!*'

This set them on singing, and Roaring Billy insisted on bawling out at the top of his stentorian lungs the doleful ditty of 'Lord Bateman and his Daughters,' which ran to thirty verses, and lasted half-an-hour. Hardly were the last words out of his mouth, when an impatient wight struck up the 'Leathern Bottel,' and heartily did they all join in the chorus, down to where the ballad describes the married man wanting to beat his wife, and using a glass bottle for the purpose, which broke and let all the wine about:—

> '*Whereas it had been the Leathern Bottel,*
> *The stopper been in he might banged away well,*'

without danger of creating an unanswerable argument in favour of leathern bottles.

By this time they were pretty well 'boozed.' A thick cloud of tobacco-smoke filled the kitchen. Heads were rolling about from side to side and arms stretched over the tables among the *débris* of broken pipes and in pools of spilt beer and froth. Despite these rude, unromantic surroundings, Absalom and Madge were leaning close against each other, hand-in-hand, almost silent, but looking in each other's eyes. What account takes passion of pipes or beer, smoke or drunken men, of snores and hoarse voices? None: they were oblivious of these things.

CHAPTER II

A MONTH after the 'hay home' a gaily dressed party passed through the fields towards the village church. Absalom and Madge went first, arm-in-arm; followed by Roaring Billy, who was to give the bride away, with his lady beside him. Behind these came two or three more couples, and last of all, toiling along by herself, an old woman, bent nearly in double; it was Madge's mother. With laugh and light jest they pushed on merrily over the stiles and through the brown autumn grass, covered with a lacework of cobwebs. The ceremony passed off well enough, except that Billy, as best-man, made the old arches of the church echo again with his response.

Absalom had taken a cottage of Farmer Humphreys. 'I'd 'ave sooner had 'un of anybody else,' said he, 'but thur war nur anuther to be had, and it bean't such a bad 'un nither, only Measter Humphreys be hardish in the mouth.' By the which he meant that Humphreys had the reputation of being rather harsh in his dealings with his workpeople. The cottage itself, however, was pleasant enough to look upon, half thatched and half slated, with a narrow strip of flower-garden in front full of hollyhocks, sun-flowers, and wall-flowers, enclosed in a high elder-hedge. Besides which, the occupier had a prescriptive right, by custom, to a patch of potato ground in the allotments about a mile up the road. And half-a-dozen damson-trees overshadowed the back of the cottage, their branches coquetting with the roof when the wind blew.

Here the bridal party made a hearty dinner, and grew jolly and genial afterwards over several gallons of beer ordered from the 'Good Woman' inn: a sign which represented a woman minus a head, and therefore silent. It was the end of the harvest, and Absalom had plenty of money in his pocket: a week's holiday was therefore indispensable. The imbibing so much beer left a taste in the mouth next morning: this must be washed away by a visit to the barrel. Then there was a stroll to the top of a high hill in the neighbourhood, and as it was very hot, the party was obliged to 'wet their whistles' and 'wash the dust out of their throats' at every sign on the road, there and back; always backed up with a second glass for the 'good of the house.' The week wore on, and by Saturday Absalom had thoroughly emancipated himself from the traces of control. Saturday evening brought a company together at the 'Good Woman,' whom it behoved him to treat. Gallon after gallon was disposed of; Absalom, as the hero of the evening, rising higher and higher in his own estimation with every glass. At length a rude jest led to a blow. Absalom had his coat off in an instant, and felled Roaring

Billy like an ox. A row began. The landlord, jealous of his
license, turned them all out into the road, when one or
two, overcome by the fresh air on top of so much liquor,
quietly laid down in the dust. Absalom, mad with drink
and vanity, hit out right and left, and piled up three half-
stupefied fellows on top of each other, then, shouting—

‘I’m the king of the castle!’

stood up in the middle of the road, and brandishing his
arms, challenged all comers.

At that moment a pair of ponies dashed round the corner
and suddenly stopped—obstructed by half-a-dozen men
lying in the way. A tall gentleman, with a very broad
forehead, a very small nose, and a profusion of grey beard,
sprang out, and went up to the landlord, who stood at the
door.

‘Johnson,’ said he sharply, ‘this is disgraceful. What’s
that fellow’s name?’ pointing to Absalom.

The landlord of course didn’t know—was very sorry.

‘I can tell ’ee, zur,’ said a voice, almost a childish treble,
and old Tim crept out from whence he had been sipping up
the forsaken goblets. ‘It be Absalom White—it be.’

‘Very good,’ said the Reverend J. Horton, and resuming
his seat, drove on; while Absalom, shouting and stagger-
ing, marched down the road, imagining he had carried all
before him.

The Reverend J. Horton was the owner of the allotment
grounds, which he had broken up from the glebe land with
the idea of benefiting the poor. Every tenant received a
circular of rules which were to be observed. Foremost
amongst these was a rule against fighting and drinking.
Absalom next week received an intimation that he must

give up his allotment. He swore, and said it didn't matter a 'cuss,' it was autumn, and the crop was up, and he'd warrant he'd get another piece before spring somewhere. But Madge cried, for her mother had prophesied evil from this offending of the 'gentle-folk.' Absalom kissed her and went to his work.

Madge, despite these things, was happy enough. Her education had not taught her to expect great things. She went forth to her work in the morning with a light heart. Merry as a cricket, she forgot in the sunshine all the ominous forebodings of her feeble old mother. It so chanced, however, that Absalom's master could not find her employment at that season, and she therefore worked on a farm at a little distance. Madge saw little of Absalom, except at night, and then he was tired and went early to bed. Her restless spirit could not be satisfied with so little companionship. Naturally fond of admiration, she thought no harm of talking and joking with the men, and her gossips encouraged her in it. The very same 'gossips' reported her freedom to Absalom—very much exaggerated. Absalom said nothing. He was slow to understand any new idea. On her road home from her work Madge had to come down a lane with but one solitary cottage in it. It belonged to an itinerant tinker, his own property, only paying quit-rent of a shilling a year. He was a bachelor, a gipsy sort of fellow, full of fun and rollicksome mirth, better educated than the labourers, and with a store of original ideas which he had acquired in travelling about. This fellow—'Bellows,' as he was called—admired Madge exceedingly, and had tried to win her for himself, but failed. Still, what pretty woman was ever displeased with the attentions of a smart young fellow? After her marriage 'Bellows' courted her more and more. It became a 'talk,' as the country people call it. Madge, thinking her title as wife exonerated her from all remarks, perhaps allowed him to go further than she ought, but, in strict earnestness, meant no harm. These things came to Absalom's ears. He grew fonder and fonder of the public-house. Still, at home he said nothing.

It grew to be winter. One cold, frosty, but beautiful moolight night Absalom came home late from his work. He had been sent up on the hills with some sheep, and did not return till two hours after his usual time. Weary and hungry, and not in the best of tempers, he walked in. The door was ajar, and there were some embers on the hearth, but Madge was neither in sight nor call. Eager for his supper, Absalom went out, and soon learned that she had gone up to the 'Good Woman.' Madge indeed, finding he did not come home, had gone up there to look for him. 'Bellows' was there, and the landlord and he had been drinking pretty freely. No sooner did Madge come in than the landlord blew out the candle, slipped out, and locked the door with a loud guffaw, leaving the pair alone in the dark. Unable to escape, Madge sat down, and they chatted away gaily enough.

It was thus that Absalom found them. He said nothing when he learnt where Madge was, but left the house and walked back to the cottage. Alarmed at his sullen demeanour, the landlord unlocked the door. Madge flew back to the cottage.

'Ab,' said she, rushing in with an armful of sticks to make a blaze, 'you'll want your supper.'

The reply was a blow which doubled her up in a corner senseless.

Absalom sat for a while sullenly glowering over the embers, and then went to bed, leaving Madge sobbing on the bare, hard earthen floor. It was midnight before she crept to his side.

Early in the morning Absalom got up and dressed. Madge was sleeping soundly, a dark circle under each eye; she had cried herself to sleep. He went out and left her.

CHAPTER III

SIX weeks passed, and Absalom did not return. Madge went over to her mother. 'He bean't come,' she said, beginning to cry.

'I knowed a wassn't,' said the old woman, rocking herself to and fro in her low rush-bottomed chair, with her feet on the hearth, almost among the ashes. 'Thee's soon have to look out for theeself.'

'How, mother?'

'Cos I'm going to die.'

'Mother!'

'I be goin' to die,' repeated the old woman in the same calm, hard tone. A life of incessant labour had crushed all sentiment out of her—except superstition—and she faced the hard facts of existence without emotion.

Madge began to weep.

'Thee go and shut up the cottage, wench, and come and bide wi' I.'

Madge did so. In a few days the old woman took to her bed. She had it dragged out of the next room—there was but one floor—and placed near the fire, which was constantly kept up. Madge waited on her assiduously when she was not out of doors at field-work. Work was growing scarcer and scarcer as the winter advanced. The old woman slowly grew weaker and weaker, till Madge could leave her no longer. So she stayed at home, and so lost the little employment she had. One evening, when the firelight was growing low and dark shadows were flickering over the ceiling, the old woman seemed to recover a little strength, and sat up in bed.

'Madge!'

'Yes, mother.'

'Thee must promise I one thing.'

'What be it, mother?'

'As thee won't have I buried by the parish.'

Madge began to cry.

'Dost thee hear?'

'I won't.'

A long silence.

'Madge!'

'Yes, mother.'

'Thee go to the fire. Dost thee see that brick in the chimbley as sticks out a little way?'

'Yes.'

'Pull it out.'

Madge caught hold, and after a few tugs pulled the brick out.

'Put thee hand in!'

Madge thrust hand and arm into the cavity, and brought out a dirty stocking.

'Has thee got th' stocking?'

'Yes, mother.'

'Bury I wi' wots in thur, and take care o' the rest on't. Thee's want it bad enough afore th' spring comes.'

Madge replaced the stocking without examining it. She was heavy at heart.

Before morning her mother was dead.

Madge went back to her own cottage, carrying with her just a sovereign in sixpences and fourpenny-bits. She sat down and wept. No one came near her. Her former gossips, always jealous of her beauty, left her alone with her sorrow. But she knew that she could not remain idle. Something must be done. So she went out to rick-work, but there was none to be had. From farm to farm Madge wearily toiled along, meeting the same answer everywhere—'Had got more on now than they could find work for.' Madge felt exceedingly ill as she slowly wended her way homewards. Then for the first time she remembered that she must shortly become a mother.

In her weak state Madge caught cold. She shivered incessantly. The poor child could not rise from her bed in the morning, her limbs were so stiff and her head so bad. She lay there all day, crying to herself. Hunger at last, towards evening, compelled her to get up and seek food. There was only a piece of crust in the cupboard and a little lard. She was trying to masticate these when there came a tap at the door. 'Come in,' said Madge. Farmer Humphreys now appeared in the doorway. He was a short, thick man, with a shock-head of yellow hair, small grey eyes, and lips almost blue.

'There be ten weeks' rent a-owing,' said he, sitting down; 'and we don't mean to wait no longer. And there's a half-side o' bacon an' a load of faggots.'

'How much is it altogether?'

'Seventeen-and-six.'

'I ain't a-got but a pound, and Absalom bean't come whoam.'

'The vagabond—cuss 'im!'

'A bean't no vagabond,' cried Madge, firing up in defence of her husband.

'Bist thee a-goin' to pay—or bisn't?' said the fellow, beginning to bully.

Madge counted him out the money, and he left, casting an ugly leer on her as he went.

Half-a-crown remained. On that half-crown Madge lived for one whole month. The cold clung to her and grew worse. Her tongue burned and her limbs shook; it was fever as well as cold—that low aguish fever, the curse of the poor. Bread and lard day by day, bread and lard, and a little weak tea. And at the month's end the half-crown was gone: sixpence went for her last half-dozen faggots. Madge crawled upstairs and wrapped herself up in a blanket, sitting on the side of the bed. It was her miserable loneliness which troubled the poor child most. Her cough, and the cold, and want of food and firing, might have been borne had there been some one to talk to. But alone they did their work. Her form was dreadfully shrunken, her hands as thin and bony as those her old mother last stretched over the fire. The ale-house which had absorbed her husband's earnings sent her no aid in this time of distress, and he had offended the clergyman who would otherwise have found her out. It grew dusky, as the poor creature sat on the edge of the bed. Suddenly there was a hand on the latch of the door downstairs. Madge trembled with eagerness as a heavy step sounded on the floor— could it be Absalom? Her black eyes, looking larger from the paleness of her sunken cheeks, began to blaze with a new light. The steps came to the foot of the stairs and began ascending. She listened eagerly. A head of yellow hair came up through the trap-door, and the small grey eyes of young Humphreys leered on her. Disappointed and amazed, Madge remained silent. Humphreys came up and sat on the bed beside her.

'Thee's got thin,' he said, with a sort of chuckle. 'Like some grub, wouldn't ye?'

No answer. He put his hand on her shoulder and muttered something in her ear. Madge seemed scarcely to understand him, but sat staring wildly.

'I'll give thee sixpence,' said Humphreys, showing one.

Then a full sense of his dishonourable intentions, mingled with shame and disgust at his unutterable meanness, came over Madge, and rising with a flush on her cheek, she struck him with all her might. It was a feeble blow, but he was unprepared: it over-balanced him; he staggered backwards, and fell heavily down the stairs. Madge, her heart beating painfully fast, leaned back on the bed and listened. There was not a sound. A dreadful thought that he might be killed flashed across her mind. Her impulse was to go down and see, but her strength failed, and she sat down again and waited. It seemed hours before she heard him stir and, after a noise like a great dog shaking himself, with mingled curses and threats, leave the house. Then a great pain came over her. She felt as if she should die, but the greatest dread was the dread of loneliness. She staggered to the window and looked out. A boy was passing, and she told him to go to Mrs. Green's and send her down. Then she fell on the bed in a faint, with the window open and the cold, bitter, biting east wind blowing in.

It was half a mile to Mrs. Green's—one of Madge's old gossips. The boy got there in two hours. Mrs. Green was putting her baby to bed, but instantly transferred that duty to her eldest girl, and went off eager for news.

At nine that night the 'Good Woman' inn resounded with talk of Madge. Not a bite nor a drop was there in the house, according to Mrs. Green. The landlord said Absalom owed him two shillings unpaid score: he could forgive her the debt, but he couldn't give nothing. Mrs. Green went home for her supper, and returning, found

Madge conscious. She would not have the parish doctor.

'Bellows,' the tinker, had during these late months been out on an itinerant journey. He came home that night, and at the 'Good Woman' heard the news. His quick wit put him up to a plan to serve the poor girl. Early in the morning he took his pack and went through the village up to the Rev. Mr. Horton's. There, under pretence of asking for kettles to mend, he told the most dismal tale to the housemaid. At breakfast-time this was reported to Mrs. Horton. Distress at such a time was sufficient to engage any lady's attention. Mrs. Horton was a frail, tender woman, but earnest in works of charity. The ponies were ordered, and down they drove. The tale was not overdrawn. 'Not a crust in the cupboard—not a stick to light a fire: the poor creature starved, and—and—you know, coming,' said the good lady afterwards, describing the scene. 'John drove after the doctor instantly, and I stayed. Poor girl! It was still-born; and she, poor thing! we saw, could not live long.'

Madge, indeed, died the same night, totally worn out at nineteen.

And Absalom? He had gone to work on a distant railway as a navvy, and, earning good wages and able to enjoy himself nightly at the taverns, forgot poor Madge. Months went on. News travels slowly among the poor, but at last intelligence did reach him that his mother was dead and Madge starving. To do him justice, he had never thought of that, and he started at once for home, travelling on foot. But passing through a village with his bundle on his shoulders, he was arrested by a policeman who observed some blood on it. It was on the slop he had worn in the fight at the 'Good Woman,' and came only from the nose. But there had been a brutal murder in the neighbour-hood, the public mind was excited, and Absalom was remanded for inquiries. It took a fortnight to prove his identity, and by then Madge was dead.

Absalom went back to the railway and drank harder than ever. It was observed that he drank now by himself and for drinking's sake, whereas before he had only been fond of liquor with company. After a year he found his way back home. Madge was forgotten, and he easily got work. Likely young men are not so common on farms: strict inquiries are rarely made.

The last that was heard of him appeared in the local newspaper:—

'DRUNK AND DISORDERLY.—Absalom White was brought up in custody, charged with obstructing the road while in a state of intoxication. Fined five shillings and seven-and-six costs.'

PART TWO

THE COMING OF SUMMER

THE June sky is of the deepest blue when seen above the fresh foliage of the oaks in the morning before the sun has filled the heavens with his meridian light. To see the blue at its best it needs something to form a screen so that the azure may strike the eye with its fulness undiminished by its own beauty; for if you look at the open sky such a breadth of the same hue tones itself down. But let the eye rise upwards along a wall of oak spray, then at the rim the rich blue is thick, quite thick, opaque, and steeped in luscious colour. Unless, indeed, upon the high downs,— there the June sky is too deep even for the brilliance of the light, and requires no more screen than the hand put up to shade the eyes. These level plains by the Thames are different, and here I like to see the sky behind and over an oak.

About Surbiton the oaks come out into leaf earlier than in many places; this spring* there were oak-leaves appearing on April 24, yet so backward are some of them that, while all the rest were green, there were two in the hedge of a field by the Ewell road still dark within ten days of June. They looked dark because their trunks and boughs were leafless against a background of hawthorn, elm, and

*1881.

other trees in full foliage, the clover flowering under them, and May bloom on the hedge. They were black as winter, and even now, on the 1st of June, the leaves are not fully formed. The trees flowered in great perfection this spring; many oaks were covered with their green pendants, and they hung from the sycamores. Except the chestnuts, whose bloom can hardly be overlooked, the flowering of the trees is but little noticed; the elm is one of the earliest, and becomes ruddy—it is as early as the catkins on the hazel; willow, aspen, oak, sycamore, ash, all have flower or catkin—even the pine, whose fructification is very interesting. The pines or Scotch firs by the Long Ditton road hang their sweeping branches to the verge of the footpath, and the new cones, the sulphur farina, and the fresh shoots are easily seen. The very earliest oak to put forth its flowers is in a garden on Oak Hill; it is green with them, while yet the bitter winds have left a sense of winter in the air.

There is a broad streak of bright-yellow charlock—in the open arable field beyond the Common. It lights up the level landscape; the glance falls on it immediately. Field beans are in flower, and their scent comes sweet even through the dust of the Derby Day. Red heads of trifolium dot the ground; the vetches have long since been out, and are so still; along the hedges parsley forms a white fringe. The charlock seems late this year; it is generally up well before June—the first flowers by the roadside or rickyard, in a waste dry corner. Such dry waste places send up plants to flower, such as charlock and poppy, quicker than happens in better soil, but they do not reach nearly the height or size. The field beans are short from lack of rain; there are some reeds in the ditch by them, and these too are short; they have not half shot up yet, for the same reason. On the sward by the Long Ditton road the goat's-beard is up; it grows to some size there every season, but is not very common elsewhere. It is said to close its sepals at noon, and was therefore called 'Jack-go-to-bed-at-noon,' but in fact it shuts much earlier, and often does not open at all, and you may pass twenty times and not see it open. Its head is like that of the dandelion, and children blow it to see what's o'clock in the same way. It forms a large ball, and browner; dandelion seed-balls are white. The grass is dotted with them now; they give a glossy, silky appearance to the meadows. Tiny pink geranium flowers show on bunches of dusty grass; silver weed lays its yellow buttercup-like flower on the ground, placing it in the angle of the road and the sward, where the sward makes a ridge. Cockspur grass—three claws and a spur like a cock's foot—is already whitened with pollen; already in comparison, for the grasses are late to lift their heads this summer. As the petals of the May fall the young leaves appear, small and green, to gradually enlarge through the hay-time.

A slight movement of the leaves on a branch of birch shows that something living is there, and presently the little head and neck of a whitethroat peers over them, and then under, looking above and beneath each leaf, and then with a noiseless motion passing on to the next. Another whitethroat follows immediately, and there is not a leaf forgotten nor a creeping thing that can hide from them. Every tree and every bush is visited by these birds, and others of the insect-feeders; the whole summer's day they are searching, and the caterpillar, as it comes down on a thread, slipping from the upper branches, only drops into their beaks. Birds, too, that at other periods feed on grain and seed, now live themselves, and bring up their young, upon insects.

I went to look over a gate to see how the corn was

rising—it is so short, now in June, that it will not hide a
hare—and on coming near there was a cock chaffinch
perched on the top, a fine bird in full colour. He did not
move though I was now within three yards, nor till I could
have almost touched him did he fly; he had a large caterpillar in his beak, and no doubt his nest or the young from
it were in the hedge. In feeding the young birds the old
ones always perch first at a short distance, and after
waiting a minute proceed to their fledgelings. Should a
blackbird come at full speed across the meadow and stay
on a hedge-top, and then go down into the mound, it is
certain that his nest is there. If a thrush frequents a tree,
flying up into the branches for a minute and then descend-
ing into the underwood, most likely the young thrushes
are there.

Little indeed do the birds care for appropriate surroundings; anything does for them, they do not aim at effect. I
heard a titlark singing his loudest, and found him perched
on the edge of a tub, formed of a barrel sawn in two, placed
in the field for the horses to drink from, as there was no
pond. Some swallows are very fond of a notice-board
fastened to a pole beside the Hogsmill bank. Upon its
upper edge they perch and twitter sweetly. There is a
muddy pond by Tolworth Farm, near the road; it is
muddy because a herd of cows drink from and stand in it,
stirring up the bottom. An elm overhangs it, and the lower
boughs are dead and leafless. On these there are always
swallows twittering over the water. Grey and yellow
wagtails run along the verge. In the morning the flock of
goslings who began to swim in the pond, now grown
large and grey, arrange themselves in a double row, some
twenty or thirty of them, in loose order, tuck their bills
under their wings and sleep. Two old birds stand in the

rear as if in command of the detachment. A sow, plastered with mud like the rhinoceri in the African lakes, lies on the edge of the brown water, so nearly the hue of the water and the mire, and so exactly at their juncture, as to be easily overlooked. But the sweet summer swallows sing on the branches; they do not see the wallowing animal, they see only the sunshine and the summer, golden buttercups and blue sky.

In the hollow at Long Ditton I had the delight, a day or two since, to see a kingfisher. There is a quiet lane, and at the bottom, in a valley, two ponds, one in enclosed grounds, the other in a meadow opposite. Standing there a minute to see if there was a martin among the birds with which the pond in the grounds is thickly covered, something came shooting straight towards me, and swerving only a yard or two to pass me, a kingfisher went by. His blue wings, his ruddy front, the white streak beside his neck, and long bill, were all visible for a moment; then he was away straight over the meadow, the directness of his course enabling it to be followed for some time till he cleared the distant hedge, probably going to visit his nest. Kingfishers, though living by the stream, often build a good way from the water. The months have lengthened into years since I saw one here before, sitting on the trunk of a willow which bends over the pond in the mead. The tree rises out of the water and is partly in it; it is hung with moss, and the kingfisher was on the trunk within a foot or so of the surface. After that there came severe winters, and till now I did not see another here. So that the bird came upon me unexpectedly out from the shadow of the trees that overhang the water, past me, and on into the sunshine over the buttercups and sorrel of the field.

This hollow at Long Ditton is the very place of singing

birds; never was such a place for singing—the valley is full of music. In the oaks blackbirds whistle. You do not often see them; they are concealed by the thick foliage up on high, for they seek the top branches, which are more leafy; but once now and then they quietly flutter across to another perch. The blackbird's whistle is very human, like a human being playing the flute; an uncertain player, now drawing forth a bar of a beautiful melody and then losing it again. He does not know what quiver or what turn his note will take before it ends; the note leads him and completes itself. It is a song which strives to express the singer's keen delight, the singer's exquisite appreciation of the loveliness of the days; the golden glory of the meadow, the light, the luxurious shadows, the indolent clouds reclining on their azure couch. Such thoughts can only be expressed in fragments, like a sculptor's chips thrown off as the inspiration seizes him, not mechanically sawn to a set line. Now and again the blackbird feels the beauty of the time, the large white daisy stars, the grass with yellow-dusted tips, the air which comes so softly unperceived by any precedent rustle of the hedge, the water which runs slower, held awhile by rootlet, flag, and forget-me-not. He feels the beauty of the time and he must say it. His notes come like wild flowers, not sown in order. The sunshine opens and shuts the stops of his instrument. There is not an oak without a blackbird, and there are others afar off in the hedges. The thrushes sing louder here than anywhere; they really seem to have louder notes; they are all round. Thrushes appear to vary their songs with the period of the year; they sing loudly now, but more plaintively and delicately in the autumn. Warblers and willow wrens sing out of sight among the trees; they are easily hidden by a leaf; ivy-leaves are so smooth, with an enamelled surface, that high up, as the wind moves them, they reflect the sunlight and scintillate. Greenfinches in the elms never cease love-making, and love-making needs much soft talking. There is a nightingale in a bush by the lane which sings so loud the hawthorn seems to shake with the vigour of his song; too loud, though a nightingale, if you stand at the verge of the boughs, as he would let you without alarm; farther away it becomes sweet and softer. Yellow-hammers call from the trees up towards the arable fields. There are but a few of them: it is the place of singing birds.

The doves in the copse are nearer the house this year; I see them more often in the field at the end of the garden. As the dove rises the white fringe on the tip of the tail becomes visible, especially when flying up into a tree. One afternoon one flew up into a hornbeam close to the garden, beside it in fact, and perched there full in view, not twenty yards at farthest. At first he sat upright, raising his neck and watching us in the garden; then, in a minute or so, turned and fluttered down to his nest. The wood-pigeons are more quiet now; their whoo-hoo-ing is not so frequently heard. By the sounds up in the elms at the top of the Brighton road (at the end of Langley Lane) the young rooks have not yet all flown, though it is the end of the first week in June. There is a little pond near the rookeries, and by it a row of elms. From one of these a heavy bough has just fallen without the least apparent cause. There is no sign of lightning, nor does it even look decayed; the wood has fractured short off; it came down with such force that the ends of the lesser branches are broken and turned up, though, as it was the lowest limb, it had not far to fall, showing the weight of the timber. There has been no hurricane of wind, nothing at all to cause it, yet this thick bough snapped. No other tree is subject to these dangerous falls of immense limbs, without warning or apparent cause, so that it is not safe to rest under elms. An accident might not occur once in ten years; nevertheless the risk is there. Elms topple over before gales which scarcely affect other trees, or only tear off a few twigs. Two have thus been thrown recently—within eighteen months—in the fields opposite Tolworth Farm. The elm drags up its own roots, which are often only a fringe round its butt, and leaves a hollow in the earth, as if it had been simply stood on end and held by these guy-ropes. Other trees do, indeed, fall in course of time, but not till they are obviously on the point of tottering, but the elm goes down in full pride of foliage. By this pond there is a rough old oak, which is the peculiar home of some titmice; they were there every day, far back on the frost and snow, and their sharp notes sounded like some one chipping the ice on the horse-pond with an iron instrument. Probably, before now, they have had a nest in a crevice.

The tallest grass yet to be seen is in a little orchard on the right-hand side of the Long Ditton road. This little orchard is a favourite spot of mine, meaning, of course, to look at: it is a natural orchard and left to itself. The palings by the road are falling, and held up chiefly by the brambles and the ivy that has climbed up them. There are trees on the left and trees on the right; a fine spruce fir at the back. The apple-trees are not set in straight lines; they were at first, but some have died away and left an irregularity. The trees themselves lean this way and that; they are scarred and marked, as it were, with lichen and moss. It is the home of birds. A blackbird had a nest this spring in the bushes on the left side, a nightingale in the bushes on the right side, and there he sang and sang for hours every morning. A sharp, relentless shrike lives in one of the trees close by, and is perpetually darting across the road upon insects on the sward among the fern there. There are several thrushes who reside in this orchard besides the lesser birds. Swallows sometimes twitter from the tops of the apple-trees. As the grass is so safe from intrusion, one of the earliest buttercups flowers here. The apple-bloom appears rosy on the bare boughs only lately scourged by the east wind. After a time the trees are in full bloom, set about into the green of the hedges and bushes and the dark spruce behind. Bennets, the flower of the grass, come up. The first bennet is to green things what a swallow is to the breathing creatures of summer. White horse-chestnut blooms stand up in their stately way, lighting the path, which is strewn with fallen oakflower. May appears on the hawthorn: there is an early bush of it. Now the grass is so high the flowers are lost under it; even the buttercups are overtopped; and soon as the young apples take form and shape white bramble-bloom will cover the bushes by the palings. Acorns will show in the oaks: the berries will ripen from red to black beneath. Along the edge of the path, where the dandelions and plantains are thick with seed, the greenfinches will come down and select those they like best: this they often do by the footpath beside the road. Lastly, the apples become red; the beech in the corner has an orange spray, and cones hang long and brown upon the spruce. The thrushes after silence sing again, and autumn approaches. But, pass when you may, this little orchard has always something, because it is left to itself—I had written neglected. I struck the word out, for this is not neglect, this is true attention, to leave it to itself, so that the young trees trail over the bushes and stay till the berries fall of their own over-ripeness, if perchance spared by the birds; so that the dead brown leaves lie and are not

swept away unless the wind pleases; so that all things
follow their own course and bent. Almost opposite, by
autumn, when the reapers are busy with the sheaves,
the hedge is white with the large trumpet-flowers of the
greater convolvulus. The hedgerow seems made of convolvulus then, nothing but convolvulus; nowhere else
does the flower flourish so strongly, and the bines remain
till the following spring. This little orchard, without a
path through it, without a border, or a parterre, or a
terrace, is a place to sit down and dream in, notwithstanding that it touches the road, for thus left to itself it has
acquired an atmosphere of peace and stillness such as be-
longs to and grows up in woods and far-away coombs of
the hills. A stray passer-by would go on without even
noticing it, it is so commonplace and unpretentious,
merely a corner of meadow irregularly dotted with apple-
trees; a place that needs frequent glances and a dreamy
mood to understand as the birds understand it. They are
always here, even in the winter, starlings and blackbirds
particularly, who resort to a kind of furrow there, which,
even in frost, seems to afford them some food. In the
spring thrushes move along, rustling the fallen leaves as
they search behind the arum-sheaths unrolling beside the
palings, or under the shelter of the group of trees where
arum-roots are plentiful. There are nooks and corners
from which shy creatures can steal out from the shadow
and be happy. The dew falls softly, more noiseless than
snow, and a star shines to the north over the spruce fir. By
day there is a loving streak of sunshine somewhere among
the tree-trunks; by night a star above. The trees are nothing to speak of in size or height, but they seem always to
bloom well and to be fruitful; treeclimbers run up these
and then go off to the elms.

Beside the Long Ditton road, up the gentle incline on the left side, the broad sward is broken by thickets and brake like those of a forest. If a forest were cleared, as those in America are swept away before the axe, but a line of underwood left beside the highway, the result would be much the same as may be seen here when the bushes and fern are in perfection. Thick hawthorn bushes stand at unequal distances surrounded with brake; one with a young oak in the centre. Fern extends from one thicket to the other, and brambles fence the thorns, which are themselves well around. From such coverts the boar was started in old English days, the fawns hide behind and about them even now in many a fair park, and where there are no deer they are frequented by hares. So near the dust which settles on them as the wheels raise it, of course, every dog that passes runs through, and no game could stay an hour, but they are the exact kind of cover game like. One morning this spring, indeed, I noticed a cock-pheasant calmly walking along the ridge of a furrow in the ploughed field, parted from these bushes by the hedge. He was so near the highway that I could see the ring about his neck. I have seen peewits or green plovers in the same field, which is now about to be built on. But though no game could stay an hour in such places, lesser birds love them, whitethroats build there, gold-crests come down from the dark pines opposite—they seem fond of pines—yellow-hammers sit and sing on them, and they are visited all day long by one or another. The little yellow flowers of tormentil are common in the grass as autumn approaches, and grasshoppers, which do not seem plentiful here, sing there. Some betony flowers are opposite on the other sward. There is a marshy spot by one of the bushes where among the rushes various semi-aquatic grasses grow.

Blackberries are thick in favourable seasons—like all fruit, they are an uncertain crop; and hawkweeds are there everywhere on the sward towards the edge. The peculiar green of fern, which is more of a relief to the eye than any other shrub with which I am acquainted, so much so that I wonder it is not more imitated, is remarkable here when the burning July sun shines on the white dust thus fringed. By then trees are gone off in colour, the hedges are tired with heat, but the fern is a soft green which holds the glance. This varies much with various seasons; this year the fern is particularly late from a lack of moisture, but sometimes it is really beautiful between these bushes. It is cut down in its full growth by those who have charge of the road, and the scene is entirely destroyed for the remainder of the season; it is not often that such bushes and such fern are found beside the highway, and, if not any annoyance to the residents, are quite as worthy of preservation (not 'preservation' by beadle) as open spaces like commons. Children, and many of larger growth, revel about them, gathering the flowers in spring and summer, the grasses and the blackberries in autumn. It is but a strip of sward, but it is as wild as if in the midst of a forest. A pleasure to every one—therefore destroy it.

In the evening from the rise of the road here I sometimes hear the cry of a barn owl skirting the hedge of Southborough Park, and disappearing under the shadow of the elms that stand there. The stars appear and the whole dome of the summer night is visible, for in a level plain like this a slight elevation brings the horizon into view. Without moon the June nights are white; a faint white light shows through the trees of Southborough Park northwards; the west has not lost all its tint over the Ditton hollow; white flowers stand in the grass; white road, white flint-heaps even, white clouds, and the stars, too, light without colour.

By day the breeze comes south and west, free over fields, over corn and grass and hedgerow; so slight a mound as this mere rise in the river-side plain lifts you up into the current of the air. Where the wind comes the sunlight is purer.

The sorrel is now high and ripening in the little meadows beside the road just beyond the orchard. As it ripens the meadow becomes red, for the stalks rise above the grass. This is the beginning of the feast of seeds. The sorrel ripens just as the fledgelings are leaving the nest; if you watch the meadow a minute you will see the birds go out to it, now flying up a moment and then settling again. After a while comes the feast of grain; then another feast of seeds among the stubble, and the ample fields, and the furze of the hills; then berries, and then winter, and the last seed.

A June rose. Something caught my eye on the top of the high hawthorn hedge beside the Brighton road one evening as it was growing dusk, and on looking again there was a spray of briar in flower, two roses in full bloom and out of reach, and one spray of three growing buds. So it is ever with the June rose. It is found unexpectedly, and when you are not looking for it. It is a gift, not a discovery, or anything earned—a gift like love and happiness. With ripening grasses the rose comes, and the rose is summer: till then it is spring. On the green banks—waste places— beside the 'New Road' (Kingsdown Road formerly) the streaked pink convolvulus is in flower; a sign that the spring forces have spent themselves, that the sun is near his fulness. The flower itself is shapely, yet it is not quite welcome; it says too plainly that we are near the meridian.

There are months of warmth to follow—brilliant sunshine
and new beauties; but the freshness, the joyous looking
forward of spring is gone. Upon these banks the first
coltsfoot flowers in March, the first convolvulus in summer, and almost the last hawkweed in autumn. A yellow
vetchling, too, is now opening its yellow petals beside the
Long Ditton road: another summer flower, which comes
in as the blue veronica is leaving the sward.

As tall as the young corn the mayweed fringes the arable
fields with its white rays and yellow centre, somewhat as
the broad moon-daisies stand in the grass. By this time
generally the corn is high above the mayweed, but this
year the flower is level with its shelter. The pale corn
buttercup is in flower by the New Road, not in the least
overshadowed by the crops at the edge of which it grows.
By the stream through Tolworth Common spotted
persicaria is rising thickly, but even this strong-growing
plant is backward and checked on the verge of the
shrunken stream. The showers that have since fallen have
not made up for the lack of the April rains, which in the
most literal sense cause the flowers of May and June.
Without those early spring rains the wild flowers cannot
push their roots and develop their stalks in time for the
summer sun. The sunshine and heat finds them unprepared. In the ditches the square-stemmed figwort is con-
spicuous by its dark green. It is very plentiful about Surbiton. Just outside the garden in a waste corner the yellow
flowers of celandine are overhung by wild hops and white
bryony, two strong plants of which have climbed up the
copse hedge, twining in and out each other. Both have
vine-like leaves; but the hops are wrinkled, those of the
bryony hairy or rough to the touch. The hops seem to be
the most powerful, and hold the bryony in the back-

ground. The young spruce firs which the wood-pigeon visited in the spring with an idea of building there look larger and thicker now the fresh green needles have appeared.

In the woodland lane to Claygate the great elder-bushes are coming into flower, each petal a creamy-white. The dogwood, too, is opening, and the wild guelder-roses there are in full bloom. There is a stile from which a path leads across the fields thence to Hook. The field by the stile was fed off in spring, and now is yellow with birdsfoot lotus, which tints it because the grass is so short. From the grass at every footstep a crowd of little 'hoppers' leap in every direction, scattering themselves hastily abroad. The little mead by the copse here is more open to the view this year, as the dry winter has checked the growth of ferns and rushes. There is a flock of missel-thrushes in it: the old birds feed the young, who can fly well in the centre of the field. Lesser birds come over from the hedges to the bunches of rushes. Slowly wandering along the lane and looking over the mound on the right hand (cow-wheat with yellow lip is in flower on the mound), there are glimpses between the bushes and the Spanish chestnut-trees of far-away blue hills—blue under the summer sky.

THE GOLDEN-CRESTED WREN

THIS lovely little bird is so small and light that it can cling suspended on the end of a single narrow leaf, or needle of pine, and it does not depress the least branch on which it may alight. The gold-crest frequents the loneliest heath, the deepest pine wood, and the immediate neighbourhood of dwellings indifferently. A Scotch fir or pine grew so near a house in which I once lived that the boughs almost brushed the window, and when confined to my room by illness, it gave me much pleasure to watch a pair of these wrens who frequently visited the tree. They are also fond of thick thorn hedges, and, like all birds, have their favourite localities, so that if you see them once or twice in one place you should mark the tree or bush, for there they are almost certain to return. It would be quite possible for a person to pass several years in the country and never see one of these birds. There is a trick in finding birds' nests, and a trick in seeing birds. The first I noticed was in an orchard; soon after, I found a second in a yew-tree (close to a window), and after that constantly came upon them as they crept through brambles or in hedgerows, or a mere speck up in a fir-tree. So soon as I had seen one I saw plenty.

AN EXTINCT RACE

THERE is something very mournful in a deserted house, and the feeling is still further intensified if it happens to have once been a school, where a minor world played out its little drama, and left its history written on the walls. For a great boys' school is like a kingdom with its monarchs, its ministers, and executioners, and even its changes of dynasty. Such a house stood no long while since on the northern border-land of Wilts and Berks, a mansion in its origin back in the days of Charles II., and not utterly unconnected with the great events of those times, but which, for hard on a hundred years—from the middle of the eighteenth to the middle of the nineteenth century— was used as a superior grammar-school, or college, as it would now be called. Gradually falling in reputation, and supplanted by modern rivals for fifteen or twenty years, the huge hollow halls and endless dormitories were silent, and the storms that sway with savage force down from the hills wreaked their will upon the windows and the rotting roof. Inside the refectory—the windows being blown in— and over the antique-carved mantelpiece, two swallows' nests had been built to the ceiling or cornice. The white-washed walls were yellow and green with damp, and covered with patches of saltpetre efflorescence. But they still bore, legible and plain, the hasty inscriptions scrawled on them, years and years before, by hands then young, but by now returned to dust. The history of this little kingdom the hopes and joys, the fears and hatreds of the subjects, still remained, and might be gathered from these writings on the walls, just as are the history of Egypt and of Assyria now deciphered from the palaces and tombs. Here were the names of the kings—the head-masters—generally with some rough doggerel verse, not often very flattering, and illustrated with outline portraits. Here were caricatures of the ushers and tutors, hidden in some corner of the dormitories once, no doubt, concealed by the furniture, coupled with the very freest personalities, mostly in pencil, but often done with a burnt stick. Dates were scattered everywhere—not often the year, but the day of the month, doubtless memorable from some expedition or lark played off half a century since. Now and then there was a quotation from the classics—one describing the groaning and shouting of the dying Hercules, till the rocks and the sad hills resounded, which irresistibly suggested the idea of a thorough caning. Other inscriptions were a mixture of Latin and any English words that happened to rhyme, together producing the most extraordinary jumble. Where now are the merry hearts that traced these lines upon the plaster in an idle mood? Attached to the mansion was a great garden, or rather wilderness, with yew hedges ten feet high and almost as thick, a splendid filbert walk, an orchard, with a sun-dial. It is all—mansion and garden, noble yew-tree hedges and filbert walk, sun-dial and all—swept away now. The very plaster upon which generation after generation of boys recorded their history has been torn down, and has crumbled into dust. Greater kingdoms than this have disappeared since the world began, leaving not a sign even of their former existence.

ORCHIS MASCULA

THE *Orchis mascula* grew in the brook corner, and in early spring sent up a tall spike of purple flowers. This plant stood alone in an angle of the brook and a hedge, within sound of water ceaselessly falling over a dam. In those days it had an aspect of enchantment to me; not only on account of its singular appearance, so different from other flowers, but because in old folios I had read that it would call up the passion of love. There was something in the root beneath the sward which could make a heart beat faster. The common modern books—I call them common of *malice prepense*—were silent on these things. Their dry and formal knowledge was without interest, mere lists of petals and pistils, a dried herbarium of plants that fell to pieces at the touch of the fingers. Only by chipping away at hard old Latin, contracted and dogged in more senses than one, and by gathering together scattered passages in classic authors, could anything be learned. Then there arose another difficulty, how to identify the magic plants? The same description will very nearly fit several flowers, especially when not actually in flower; how determine which really was the true root? The uncertainty and speculation kept up the pleasure, till at last I should not have cared to have had the original question answered. With my gun under my arm I used to look at the orchis from time to time, so long as the spotted leaves were visible, till the grass grew too long.

THE LIONS IN TRAFALGAR SQUARE

THE lions in Trafalgar Square are to me the centre of London. By those lions began my London work; from them, as spokes from the middle of a wheel, radiate my London thoughts. Standing by them and looking south you have in front the Houses of Parliament, where resides the mastership of England; at your back is the National Gallery—that is art; and farther back the British Museum—books. To the right lies the wealth and luxury of the West End; to the left the roar and labour, the craft and gold, of the City. For themselves, they are the only monument in this vast capital worthy of a second visit as a monument. Over the entire area covered by the metropolis there does not exist another work of art in the open air. There are many structures and things, no other art. The outlines of the great animals, the bold curves and firm touches of the master hand, the deep indents, as it were, of his thumb on the plastic metal, all the *technique* and grasp written there, is legible at a glance. Then comes the *pose* and expression of the whole, the calm strength in repose, the indifference to little things, the resolute view of great ones. Lastly, the soul of the maker, the spirit which was taken from nature, abides in the massive bronze. These lions are finer than those that crouch in the cages at the Zoological Gardens; these are truer and more real, and, besides, these are lions to whom has been added the heart of a man. Nothing disfigures them; smoke and, what is much worse, black rain—rain which washes the atmosphere of the suspended mud—does not affect them in the least. If the choke-damp of fog obscures them, it leaves no stain on the design; if the surfaces be stained, the idea made tangible in metal is not. They are no more touched than Time itself by the alternations of the seasons. The only noble open-air work of native art in the four-million city, they rest there supreme and are the centre. Did such a work exist now in Venice, what immense folios would be issued about it! All the language of the studios would be huddled together in piled-up and running-over laudation, and curses on our insular swine-eyes that could not see it. I have not been to Venice, therefore I do not pretend to a knowledge of that mediaeval potsherd; this I do know, that in all the endless pictures on the walls of the galleries in London, year after year exposed and disappearing like snow somewhere unseen, never has there appeared one with such a subject as this. Weak, feeble, mosaic, gim-crack, coloured tiles, and far-fetched compound monsters, artificial as the graining on a deal front door, they cannot be compared; it is the gingerbread gilt on a circus car to the column of a Greek temple. This is pure open air, grand as Nature herself, because it *is* Nature with, as I say, the heart of a man added.

But if any one desire the meretricious painting of warm light and cool yet not hard shade, the effect of colour, with the twitching of triangles, the spangles glittering, and all the arrangement contrived to take the eye, then he can have it here as well as noble sculpture. Ascend the steps to the National Gallery, and stand looking over the balustrade down across the square in summer hours. Let the sun have sloped enough to throw a slant of shadow outward; let the fountains splash whose bubbles restless speak of rest and leisure, idle and dreamy; let the blue-tinted pigeons nod their heads walking, and anon crowd through the air to the roof-tops. Shadow upon the one side, bright light upon the other, azure above the swallows. Ever rolling the human stream flows, mostly on the south side yonder, near enough to be audible, but toned to bearableness. A stream of human hearts, every atom a living mind filled with what thoughts?—a stream that ran through Rome once, but has altered its course and wears away the banks here now and triturates its own atoms, the hearts, to dust in the process. Yellow omnibuses and red cabs, dark shining carriages, chestnut horses, all rushing, and by their motion mixing their colours so that the commonness of it disappears and the hues remain, a streak drawn in the groove of the street—dashed hastily with thick camel's hair. In the midst the calm lions, dusky, unmoved, full always of the one grand idea that was infused into them. So full of it that the golden sun and the bright wall of the eastern houses, the shade that is slipping towards them, the sweet swallows and the azure sky, all the human stream holds of wealth and power and coroneted panels—nature, man, and city—pass as naught. Mind is stronger than matter. The soul alone stands when the sun sinks, when the shade is universal night, when the van's wheels are silent and the dust rises no more.

At summer noontide, when the day surrounds us and it is bright light even in the shadow, I like to stand by one of the lions and yield to the old feeling. The sunshine glows on the dusky creature, as it seems, not on the surface, but under the skin, as if it came up from out of the limb. The roar of the rolling wheels sinks and becomes distant as the sound of a waterfall when dreams are coming. All the abundant human life is smoothed and levelled, the abruptness of the individuals lost in the flowing current, like separate flowers drawn along in a border, like music heard so far off that the notes are molten and the theme only remains. The abyss of the sky over and the ancient sun are near. They only are close at hand, they and immortal thought. When the yellow Syrian lions stood in old time of Egypt, then, too, the sunlight gleamed on the eyes of men, as now this hour on mine. The same consciousness of light, the same sun, but the eyes that saw it and mine, how far apart! The immense lion here beside me expresses larger nature—cosmos—the ever-existent thought which sustains the world. Massiveness exalts the mind till the vast roads of space which the sun tramples are as an arm's-length. Such a moment cannot endure long; gradually the roar deepens, the current resolves into individuals, the houses return—it is only a square.

But a square potent. For London is the only *real* place in the world. The cities turn towards London as young partridges run to their mother. The cities know that they are not real. They are only houses and wharves, and bricks and stucco; only outside. The minds of all men in them, merchants, artists, thinkers, are bent on London. Thither they go as soon as they can. San Francisco thinks London; so does St. Petersburg.

Men amuse themselves in Paris; they work in London. Gold is made abroad, but London has a hook and line on every napoleon and dollar, pulling the round discs hither. A house is not a dwelling if a man's heart be elsewhere. Now, the heart of the world is in London, and the cities with the simulacrum of man in them are empty. They are moving images only; stand here and you are real.

All Futura Books are available at your bookshop or newsagent, or can be ordered from the following address:
Futura Books, Cash Sales Department,
P.O. Box 11, Falmouth, Cornwall.

Please send cheque or postal order (no currency), and allow 40p for postage and packing for the first book plus 18p for the second book and 13p for each additional book ordered up to a maximum charge of £1.49 in U.K.

Customers in Eire and B.F.P.O. please allow 40p for the first book, 18p for the second book plus 13p per copy for the next 7 books, thereafter 7p per book.

Overseas customers please allow 60p for postage and packing for the first book and 18p per copy for each additional book.